OWNED BY AN AUSSIE

True Stories About Living With An Australian Shepherd

Megan Grandinetti

Publication Data

Megan Grandinetti

Editors: Lois Tuffin and Margarita Martinez

Owned by an Aussie - True Stories about Living with an Australian Shepherd – First edition

Summary: "Real stories about living with an Australian Shepherd as told by Aussie owners" – Provided by publisher.

ISBN: 978-1-954288-16-4

[1. Australian Shepherds – Non-Fiction] I. Title.

This book has been written with the published intent to provide accurate and author-itative information in regard to the subject matter included. While every reasonable precaution has been taken in preparation of this book the author and publisher expressly disclaim responsibility for any errors, omissions, or adverse effects arising from the use or application of the information contained inside. The techniques and suggestions are to be used at the reader's discretion and are not to be considered a substitute for professional veterinary care. If you suspect a medical problem with your dog, consult your veterinarian.

Design by Sorin Rădulescu
First paperback edition, 2021

TABLE OF CONTENTS

Introduction

Ever wondered what it's really like to own an Australian Shepherd? While you may have already heard about their inquisitive nature and mental agility, there is so much more to these dogs. Aussies have emotional intelligence, playfulness, and loyalty in spades. They bring so much magic, fun, and mischief into your life that you will find it almost impossible to switch to another type of dog after having one of these canines snuggle right into your heart.

This is not a guide about raising an Australian Shepherd. Instead, we give you an in-depth look at what it really means to own an Aussie, with all the joy, laughter, frustration, and landmines of chewed-up toys in your potential future. We have interviewed hundreds of Australian Shepherd owners to hear the stories of their pets' quirky characteristics, then picked the best ones to demonstrate what it's like to own, live with, and train, with these unique dogs.

Since Australian Shepherds totally commit to their owners, they also love working for you! They might make themselves indispensable on a farm, or they could serve as heartwarmingly sweet physical and emotional support dogs. Here's a bit of a warning though: if Aussies don't have enough work (or play) to keep them occupied, they can also get into a bit of trouble, so make sure you give your Aussie a job.

For this book, we interviewed dozens of individuals and families who described their Aussies as guardians, helpers, and best friends. Prepare to laugh out loud, shed a tear or two, and possibly roll your eyes in empathy as you read through the pages ahead. Go ahead! Enjoy the sentimental journey that comes with sharing your life and home with an Australian Shepherd or two—in one case, even four!

Along the way, you'll learn about nine breed behaviors, personality characteristics, and unexpected quirks that are unique to Australian Shepherds. They are intuitive learners; affectionate, close companions; high-energy cyclones of playfulness; hard-working allies; devoted family members; loyal protectors; creatures of habit; sensitive souls; and hoarders of toys. As you will see, even after messier incidents, their owners cannot stay angry when they see that infamous stub of a tail wagging in front of them.

This book aims to give you a good starting place to understand the characteristics, behaviors, and quirks of Aussies, and how owning one can completely change your life for the better.

Chapter 1:
Intuitive Learners

Many longtime pet parents describe their furry best friends as "practically human" in terms of their emotional intelligence and problem-solving skills. This is especially true in the case of Australian Shepherds, to a point that can be either life-saving or aggravating.

Australian Shepherds are exceptionally smart. From understanding human speech to learning the house rules and how to open doors, Aussies are masters of ingenuity and communication—whether their owners like it or not. That's what makes training these dogs so vital to living with them harmoniously. By keeping them busy and giving them ways to contribute, you make Aussies feel like valued members of the family.

The Australian Shepherd owners we interviewed described their dogs' uncanny ability to learn without being taught and to figure out things that seem well outside of the abilities of other dogs.

Zoe "Finds It" on the Farm

Jori Caswell capitalizes on the talents of her Aussie, Zoe, to find her chickens and shorten her workdays on the farm.

I'm a small farmer who keeps horses and raises cage-free chicken for eggs. This can be a bit of a handful, especially when chickens decide not to come back to the coop at night to stay safe from predators.

I'd heard that Australian Shepherds were great working dogs and highly intelligent, so I decided to put this to the test with my Aussie,

Zoe. It took very little training for her to realize I wanted her to go out, find my wayward chickens, and herd them back to the coop.

At first, I would spot the chicken and direct Zoe toward it, telling her to "find the chicken." I'd praise her lavishly when she brought the bird back to me, and within a few repetitions of this routine, closing up the chickens at night became so much easier!

I no longer have to stomp through the long grass, climb over gates, and peer into every hole and hollow that a small chicken could fit into. I just tell Zoe "find the chicken," and she does most of the work—all while finding the task of hunting down the birds much more enjoyable than I ever did! Zoe cuts down our chicken-herding time so much that now I'm rarely ever late for appointments because I'm searching around the farm for a stubborn bird. This used to be a routine occurrence!

What amazes me most is that Zoe has learned the chickens' favorite hiding spots. She'll check the places where we've found birds in the past first before moving on to a general sweep of the property.

She'll stick to the task for as long as it takes—sometimes more than 15 minutes. Zoe is never satisfied until she has "found it" and "won" the game!

Sometimes Zoe will find chickens that I hadn't even realized were missing, striking a pointing pose to show me where they are or herding the squawking little birds around the corner of the henhouse. She knows now that when it starts to get dark, the chickens are supposed to be inside—and it gives her an excuse to run around the property, playing "fetch!"

Once I realized how good Zoe was at locating chickens, I decided to see if I could teach her to find other things. Now, whenever I want Zoe to find something, I just show her the item and do a quick practice run by setting the object on the ground and telling her to "find the _____!" I praise and reward her when she finds the item. She has learned to indicate when she's found an object by putting her paw on it. I didn't teach her that—she came up with it on her own!

Recently, some cows ran through an electric fence and popped off a bunch of the plastic clips that hold the wire to the post. I showed Zoe a clip and told her what it was—"fence clip"—then tossed it on the ground and told her to "find the fence clip." She went right to it and proceeded to sniff around the grass. My brother and I ended up spotting all the bright yellow clips ourselves, but Zoe was working so hard at her task that we made sure to leave some for her to find so she could win the game! She doesn't seem to forget the names of objects, and has no problem generalizing "find it" to new items.

A few weeks ago, we had a problem with two young roosters who didn't want to go into the coop at night. It was cold, rainy, and getting dark, but that didn't stop these birds from bolting off into a field instead of coming inside. To make matters worse, the roosters had black and gray feathers—in those conditions, I knew I'd never find them by sight alone.

Fortunately, Zoe was on the job. She followed their tracks—a task which requires running in circles and zigzags, because chickens don't walk in straight lines—and within half an hour Zoe had found one rooster and chased him into my arms. Ten minutes later she reappeared, herding the second bird right into the coop! Without Zoe's help, I would never have been able to find the runaway roosters, and they likely would have ended up as a tasty meal for a racoon or a fox.

Zoe is the first Australian Shepherd I have had, and her intelligence continually amazes me. I've never had such a useful and helpful dog. She's a sheer delight to my everyday work around the farm.

While Zoe helps out on the farm, our next Aussie has found a way to be helpful around the house, both inside and out.

Ask Jazzmine to Open the Door For You

Roxann Crosby has discovered that having an Aussie can provide another set of hands when yours are full.

I never meant to teach my Aussie, Jazzmine, to open doors, but maybe it was inevitable that she'd learn by watching me. After all, nothing escapes an Aussie's notice! Our house has doors with long handles instead of round doorknobs. Jazzmine would watch in fascination as I pulled the handles down, and the doors magically opened.

One day, Jazzmine jumped into our doggie pool and came out soaking wet. I wanted to keep the house dry, so I left her outside and

Photo Courtesy of
Roxann Crosby

closed the front door behind me while I ran into the house to get a towel. Much to my surprise, while I was at the other end of the hall, I heard the front door open! Was there an intruder in my house?

I looked around anxiously, but there were no humans. Just Jazzmine, standing in the open door with her tongue hanging out.

Curious, I dried her off, then led her outside and shut the door again, leaving her in the front yard. This time I watched as she looked up at the door handle, then reached up with her paws to turn it. In short order, the front door opened again, and she let herself inside.

From that day on, I could ask her to open doors for me if my hands were full. I was particularly grateful for Jazzmine's intelligence and skill on rainy days when I had to go grocery shopping. I loaded my arms up with as many groceries as I could carry and shouted for Jazzmine to open the door for me as I approached the house. Having her extra set of paws made life much easier!

Jazzmine was always a gentle and well-behaved dog, so her ability to open doors never caused us any problems. We used to put all our dogs into the bedroom when company came over, so our guests wouldn't have to deal with a barrage of enthusiastic barks and wagging tails. But the truth was, we only put Jazzmine in the bedroom because it didn't seem fair for her to get to meet the guests while her more rambunctious siblings weren't allowed.

She did let herself out of the bedroom once while company was over—an impressive feat since the bedroom door opened inward, so she had to press the handle down, then pull the door in toward herself. But all she did was offer a friendly tail wag before letting us lead her back to the bedroom. That time, she got the idea that she was supposed to stay inside.

Jazzmine passed on to the rainbow bridge in February 2019. We couldn't resist adding another Aussie to our family after her passing because Jazzmine was such a wonderful dog!

Ridge the Sock-Fetcher

Debra Padden regales us with the tale of how her Aussie, Ridge, learned to translate the word "sock" and to deliver!

We've known for a long time that our Australian Shepherd, Ridge, knows many verbal commands. I'll often tell him to "bring it" when we're playing together, or to "go find your _____" when one of his toys is missing. However, I never taught him to fetch my clothes—and the first time he did it, I hadn't asked him to bring it or go find them at all!

When we tell Ridge we're going to "go for a ride," he'll immediately run outside and sit by the passenger door of our truck if we let him. He also knows the word "Ranger"—the type of truck we have—and will respond to that word by running to the vehicle.

His favorite activity is when we take a ride to our cabin, where he can run at full speed and explore the endless woods. He has to stay in the yard when we're at home, but up at the cabin he is free to do as he likes. We even planted Ridge his own garden plot up by the cabin, because if we don't, he'll enthusiastically try to "help" me to harvest my vegetables—and Aussie teeth aren't the gentlest method for harvesting bean pods.

Although we've taught Ridge a lot on purpose, he still surprises us with how much he understands.

Ridge knows the word "socks" because he has a toy made of old socks, knotted together for him to chew on and drag around the house. I didn't realize he understood that these were the same items we use to keep our feet warm until one cold day, when Ridge wanted to play outside.

He was bouncing around like he always does when he wants Mom to take him for a walk, but I wasn't too enthusiastic about the idea.

Photo Courtesy of
Debra Padden

I playfully told him that it was cold outside, and I'd need to put my warm socks on if we were going to go out and play.

Lo and behold, Ridge appeared just moments later with a pair of my warmest, thickest socks held carefully between his teeth. He'd pulled them from the clean laundry basket upstairs.

I marveled as I picked up the socks—I'd never taught him that—and I no longer had an excuse not to take him outside to play!

Now that you're impressed with the sock-fetching dog, let's meet one that can spell the names of at least two daily tasks.

Arizona Learns to Spell

Lisa Hon tells us how her Aussie, Arizona, figured out how the letters of certain words equal one of her daily routines and provide two opportunities to get food.

My daughter has had three Australian Shepherd companions. Each one has been a little different in terms of temperament, but they're always smart. A few years back, my daughter talked me into adopting one of her own pups' littermates. They were just too darned cute to resist!

Arizona will be three in November. She was a very rambunctious puppy, and we knew she would need lots of training. Let the classes begin! She knows the usual commands: sit, stay, wait, crate, down, roll over, and others. But she's also learned one very unexpected thing.

When my husband is due home from work, Arizona sits in a chair by the window. When his car turns into the driveway, she starts "talking"—a very different sound from her "I see a squirrel" bark. To give her an outlet for her excitement, my husband usually asks if Arizona wants to get the mail when he opens the door to our home. Over time, Arizona has learned the word "mail"—to the point that it can be a problem.

Photo Courtesy of
Lisa Hon

On days when it rains hard, my husband will stop and get the mail from the shelter of his car to avoid having to walk all the way back down the driveway in the storm. To avoid disappointing Arizona, he'll tell me that he already got the M-A-I-L. But there's no fooling our girl: Arizona now barks excitedly at the mention of M-A-I-L, often running to the door and taking her leash in her mouth hopefully. She really wants that quality walk time with my husband, no matter what the weather is like outside!

The same thing has happened with "ice cream" and "dinner." We often talk to Arizona while preparing these daily treats, as we might talk to any pet—not expecting her to actually understand what we are saying and hold us to it!

It started with asking Arizona if she wanted dinner each night as she followed us around the kitchen eagerly while we cooked for the family and prepared her dog food. Of course the answer was always "yes!" It got to the point that she understood that the word "dinner" meant it was chow time—which meant that any time we used the word in any sentence, she would perk her ears up and come stare at us with expectant, soulful eyes.

Just like with M-A-I-L, we eventually started spelling D-I-N-N-E-R when we needed to discuss dinner plans or grocery lists without getting Arizona's hopes up. However, this only worked for a little while. D-I-N-N-E-R soon became associated in her mind with future food, and now she gets just as excited when we spell the word as when we say it.

Her latest spelling triumph so far has been I-C-E C-R-E-A-M. In the evening, my husband and I often enjoy a little ice cream with a movie after dinner. He sometimes lets Arizona lick his bowl after we are done, and Arizona loves it! To keep her from getting sick, I buy ice-cream cups made especially for dogs so that she can still enjoy a treat along with us.

Can you see where this is going? Sure enough, Arizona has learned to "ask for" ice cream after dinner each night. She'll pace between my husband and me, put her feet up on the couch or chair, and start "talking"—that quiet, complicated little bark that she uses to communicate with humans. How did this happen? Well...

Some days my husband would ask me if Arizona had been a good girl and if she could have her ice cream. She would respond to hearing "ice cream" by running into the kitchen and sitting down beside the freezer. We didn't want Arizona to eat the frozen treat every night due to health concerns, so we started spelling I-C-E C-R-E-A-M on nights when we didn't want to tempt her. Needless to say, this didn't work very well. Now I feed her a little less dog food for dinner because we know she'll talk us into letting her have her treat almost every night!

Arizona is as spoiled as she is smart because she's just so dang good at asking for what she wants. How do you ignore a pup who's sitting by the freezer, looking up at you with big blue eyes, or who runs and brings you her leash because she's so excited to get the M-A-I-L?

We've managed to keep her healthy and well-behaved with the help of obedience school, but it's definitely a lot more like living with another human than we ever expected!

Aussies don't just like to get their snacks on time; they love to be treated as members of the family when you talk to them, as you will soon see.

Captain Jack Has Attitude

Kimberly Ward has found that single-word commands do not impress her Aussies, Captain Jack and Monk, but asking them to cooperate and learn tricks certainly does.

My two Aussies, Captain Jack and Monk, are real characters. Monk is the bigger but submissive dog, while Captain Jack is a little fluffball who likes to be in charge. We didn't send them to formal obedience school because, growing up, I had lots of experience with training dogs at home. But despite the most dire predictions of some dog trainers, Captain Jack and Monk are absolute pleasures—as long as you treat them with respect.

I've always talked to my Aussies just like you would talk to human kids. Many dog owners do this, but few expect their dogs to understand! I have learned that Captain Jack and Monk will do almost anything I ask them to, as long as I ask gently and respectfully.

Commands of "Come!" or "Sit!" will be met by Captain Jack with a withering, defiant stare. If dogs could roll their eyes, I imagine that he would. However, if I ask or suggest that he do something—just like I would with a human—he'll follow even the most complex requests.

I first discovered this when encouraging Jack and Monk to take care of a bird problem we had on our deck when we lived in Hawaii. Their food bowls were kept on our deck—and they didn't always gobble up their dinners right away.

When Jack and Monk left food sitting in their bowls, local birds would descend and start devouring it. One day, in exasperation, I came outside and jokingly waved my arms toward the birds.

"Jack! Monk! Why don't you take care of your food?" I asked. "I can't afford to feed you and the birds."

I then went around to work in the back yard, not thinking anything of it. Imagine my surprise when Monk came trotting around the side of the house—with a bird he'd caught in his mouth!

Since that day, I can ask, "Why don't you go check on the birds?" and my dogs will run and disperse the flock.

If the dogs start barking for no obvious reason during the night, I open my window and talk to them. "Hey, it's nighttime now," I say.

"You don't need to be barking. Why don't you go into the garage and go to bed?" And, much to the astonishment of my neighbors, Captain Jack and Monk do just that!

I've gotten more than one stare of awe when family has watched me ask the boys: "Are you ready to go back outside now?" and they've happily trotted away to do just that.

My boys are so intelligent that, over time, friends started suggesting I enroll them in dog shows or agility competitions. I liked the idea of having a new hobby to do with my Aussies, but I wasn't sure if my older, somewhat free-spirited dogs were really cut out for the show circuit.

Photo Courtesy of Kimberly Ward

Captain Jack (Left) and Monk

Soon, however, I discovered an alternative: an online program that awarded certifications for dogs who mastered large numbers of advanced tricks.

I set to work teaching Jack and Monk the website's curriculum, and sure enough, they were thrilled with the new "game." To them learning to do a new trick successfully seemed to be a point of pride. They loved the attention I was giving them, and they loved showing off. Although they were already six years old when this training started, they achieved their advanced level trick certification, and will test for expert level by summer.

When teaching the boys a new trick, I only have to show them what to do two or three times. Then they remember it forever, and eagerly whip out their knowledge on command. As of today, they can perform more than 85 tricks—and the only reason they've stopped learning more is that, frankly, I can't think of any new ones to teach them! I often think they're smarter than I am.

Captain Jack and Monk really are like having a couple of human family members around. They'll happily comply with any suggestions or requests—as long as it's a suggestion, not an order!

* * *

As you likely noticed, these owners were surprised at how their pets intuitively learned words and actions based on watching people and absorbing their cues. This ability to integrate this information and adapting their behavior to be more helpful (and entertaining!) says so much about how clever these creatures really are.

It's clear that Aussies can be delightful companions who, with proper training, are as helpful and considerate as they are perceptive and quick-witted. Whether they are gathering up chickens or socks, opening doors or scaring away birds, your pets can help you get more done in a day, even if you have to find new ways to communicate about when you plan to eat!

To create good habits early, begin training your dog consistently as soon as they arrive in your home. They will thrive with this intellectual stimulation and attention. Keep your training sessions short and focused on one or two skills, then reward them with some play time. Not only will this build their skills, it will also help you to bond with your pet.

But just as a human family member can become quite a handful if not trained in how to be helpful and considerate, so can an Aussie. As with human companions, it may be best not to enter into a relationship with an Aussie unless you're sure that what the dog offers is what you need, and you're ready to invest the necessary time into building shared understandings that will serve you both well.

As the chapters to come will show, unusually high intelligence is not an Aussie's only unique trait. Australian Shepherds' attributes create a package that may be the perfect companion for some—but may be too much to handle for others.

Chapter 2:
Affectionate, Close Companions

Australian Shepherds are known for being constant at your side, no matter where you go. They are so constant, in fact, that they've earned the nickname "Velcro dogs." Remember, these dogs were bred to herd animals; unless you live on a farm, they will start shepherding you from place to place. Fortunately, this care for other creatures means they will be there for you on good days and bad.

The attachment Aussies form to their families can be considered by some to be almost fanatical. The downside is that they can be possessive of their owners or develop a mistrust toward strangers. The upside is that Aussies make amazingly loyal companions since they stick to their owners' sides like glue.

A common theme among Aussie owners we interviewed was, "You'll never go to the bathroom alone again." Some Aussies will check on their owners in the shower; others will be "helpful" in the kitchen, while others just want to hug you when you're having a bad day.

While some people might find an Aussie's clingy nature to be a bit too much to handle, all of the Aussie owners we interviewed are simply happy to have them by their sides, or at their feet, or wherever they go.

Never Lonely With an Aussie

Rebecca Swyers tells us about how her Aussie, Millie, has stopped her from feeling lonely while living in Phoenix, away from her friends and family.

My dog, Millie, is always near me. When I heard someone call Aussies Velcro dogs, I immediately knew what they were talking about. Some people don't like it when their dogs follow them around everywhere, but I love it!

When I turned 18, I moved from the suburbs in California to Phoenix, Arizona, for college. After a few years, I knew that Phoenix was where I wanted to live, so I got an apartment and moved out here permanently. Of course, I brought Millie to live with me, and it was the best choice I ever made. Before she came to Phoenix, life was messy and unstructured and lonely. Bringing Millie to my new home helped me to grow up. She forced me to have a routine, even on days I didn't want to. It helped my time-management skills because I had to walk her at the same time daily, especially to avoid the heat here. This made me a better employee at my job and also a better student.

Photo Courtesy of Rebecca Swyers

Living alone in the city has been hard, especially during the pandemic. Right now, I am working toward my master's degree. Due to the pandemic, I am doing my school virtually instead of in-person, which means my days are mostly filled with Millie and our walks. Now I can't seem to go anywhere by myself, and that makes me feel less lonely living in a city where I don't have many friends or family.

Now that we're in lockdown, Millie is more relaxed since I'm home all the time, but she also is even more Velcro-like than she used to be. She has even started to get upset if I lock her out of the bathroom. When I shower, she keeps checking on me to make sure I'm okay—I think because she hates taking baths. She will come into the bathroom, push the shower curtain out of the way with her nose, and stare at me for 30 seconds or so to make sure I'm okay. Once she has verified that I'm indeed alive and well, she'll go lie down then come back in a few minutes to check on me again.

Having a dog that always wants to be near me is amazing. She's my best friend, and I'm never alone. Millie is the biggest blessing!

Millie is an example of how Aussies can keep their owners from feeling lonely, even when they're in the shower. Our next Aussie takes that a bit further...

Angel the Shower Dog

Sheila Rankin's Aussie, Angel, not only checks on her in the shower: she occasionally jumps in the shower too.

My Aussie, Angel, is absolutely a Velcro dog. Anytime I leave the house (even if just for five minutes) and return, she goes crazy, greeting me with frenetic butt wiggles and grrrrring.

Normally, Angel comes into the bathroom with me and stays outside the shower. I use a clear shower curtain, so she can still keep an eye on me while I'm in there.

One day, the clear curtain wasn't enough for her. She kept pulling at the shower curtain with her nose to get a closer look. While I was rinsing my hair, I felt something touching my leg.

I looked down and realized that Angel had come into the shower with me! I laughed. Once she was there, I decided that it was a good opportunity to give her a shower too. She wasn't thrilled when that happened! She's not a huge fan of water, and she just looked back at me with an expression like, "Mom, when are we going to be finished?" She waited patiently anyway. She just wanted to be able to be with me, Velcro-ed to my side, even if it meant having to tolerate getting clean herself.

Angel still follows me into the bathroom every time, but now she stands outside the shower and just watches me.

Some Aussies will get clean just to be near you, whereas others will create quite a mess just to be underfoot.

Photo Courtesy of Shelia Rankin

Is That Grease in Your Fur?

Mary Sanders tells us about how involved Juno likes to be in the kitchen; so involved, in fact, that she often gets covered in grease.

Juno has always been my baby, and I am her mama. Wherever I go, she goes, even if it's just into the next room. When I'm in the bath, she lies on the bathmat. When I use the bathroom, she stands in the doorway. My desk chair doesn't roll anymore because of all of the clumps of fur left behind from Juno sitting under my chair.

Juno is stuck to my side so much that I have had to clean grease out of her fur multiple times from cooking with her at my feet. She was probably about two years old when the first grease incident occurred. The house we lived in at the time had a U-shaped kitchen in which two adults could barely be comfortable, let alone with a giant ball of fuzz on the floor. I had several stove burners going, with ground beef browning on a front burner. As usual, Juno's bum was against my feet as I stood in front of the stove. I must have taken a little too long to dig through the seasonings because the beef started popping crazily all over the stovetop, counter, and floor. I shooed Juno out of the kitchen while I let the beef drain in the sink, and I cleaned up the grease from the various surfaces.

I finished cooking, then had to shoo Juno out of the kitchen three more times before we sat down to eat. It wasn't long into dinner that I felt Juno walk under the table. As she brushed up against my legs, something rubbed onto my leg that was shiny, oily, and covered in Aussie hairs. I looked at Juno and noticed something slimy all over her bum.

Then it hit me—the grease from the ground beef had splattered on her! Initially I was concerned that it had burned her, but after combing through her butt fluff, it was clear that the grease had landed only on the outer layer of fur. I had heard her licking something immediately after I kicked her out of the kitchen that first time, but that, combined with me trying to wipe it off with a wet paper towel, just made the grease-fur combination worse.

Word of advice: always keep some blue liquid dish soap on hand for unexpected Aussie baths!

Luna isn't the only Aussie who gets messy in the kitchen. It turns out that being a close-up dog can lead to some serious spills.

Luna and the Thanksgiving Turkey

Eva Kory tells us an entertaining story of how Luna took her need to be on top of her owner's every move a bit too far on Thanksgiving Day.

Luna is a Velcro dog, through and through, when it comes to her favorite people. She loves the people she knows well with every single hair on her wiggly body. She starts her greeting routine by cry-ing. You can hear the wide variety of Husky-like howls, whines, and squeals before you even open the door. She then moves to wagging her entire body so hard that she at times will fall over with joy. It was a lot of hard work to train her not to jump up and lick my forehead (because Aussies can *jump*).

Her favorite display of love is following me from room to room at all times. Luna is constantly under, in between, and on top of my feet. She is a serious tripping hazard, especially in the kitchen when I'm trying to cook a meal and I have to ask her to move every time I step from the stove to the counter or the refrigerator. The list of times I've spilled or dropped things because of her is endless. Coffee, plates, soup; everything has ended up on our kitchen floor!

A few years ago, we celebrated our first Thanksgiving in our new house. It was also the first time my husband and I hosted a large group of people—so many that we needed two turkeys to feed every-one. The stakes, emotions, and anxiety were all running high.

Around 4 p.m., I finished setting the tables and went upstairs to change and get ready for our guests to arrive. Luna, of course, came with me. I couldn't decide between two outfits, and I ended up leaving the second choice on my bed.

Just five minutes before guests were supposed to arrive, I decided to bring one of the two turkeys to the table. However, Luna had other plans. She decided that the best way to stay close and ensure the safety and well-being of our turkey (and me) was to step **directly** in front of me as I was carrying the giant tray.

I would like to say that I gracefully saved myself and the turkey, but that was not the case. I went flying in the air, and so did the roasted bird. Somehow I managed to land right on top of the turkey, which ruined my carefully selected dress, as well as the turkey. Luna was also covered in turkey: our Blue Merle Aussie was a little more brown than blue that day. Luna thought the floor turkey tasted great, but I couldn't serve that to my guests.

Photo Courtesy of Eva Kory

I had just finished cleaning the turkey off the floor when a few of our guests started arriving. I hadn't had a chance to change, but those that saw me covered in food found it amusing and also predictable, knowing our dog.

I ran upstairs, changed into my second outfit, and came down with just enough time to welcome the rest of our guests. We only had one turkey to share, but it ended up providing plenty of food for everyone, along with a highly memorable Thanksgiving.

I learned two lessons that day for hosting Thanksgiving: always make two turkeys, and always pick a backup outfit just in case Luna "protects" me too carefully again.

We've learned that Aussies can cause a little trouble in the kitchen because they're slightly too involved, and our next story shows just how affectionate these helpful dogs can be.

An Aussie and Her Grandma

Pam Williams tells us about her grand-dog, Bonnie, an Aussie who loves to follow her around and lay her paw on her as a sign of affection.

Bonnie is my grand-dog. She lives a couple of blocks from me, and because we have 13 acres, her mom drops her off every morning before she goes to work.

Bonnie comes straight in and finds me and smiles the way only an Aussie can smile. If I'm sitting down, she comes and lies next to me with her paw on my arm. If we say, "Where's Pa?" she jumps down and goes to my husband. She is affectionate with him, too, and uses her paws to show it.

As a small puppy, Bonnie would sit next to me. She couldn't have been more than three months old, and I remember her laying her paw on me when we were sitting on the sofa. She loves to be given affection and anticipates that you will totally commit every minute to her.

Photo Courtesy of
Pam Williams

She normally will follow me from room to room, but if I am busy, she likes to lie on the hardwood floor, where it is cool. She never lets me get far away, and, at times, stands next to me, wanting me to sit down with her. She loves to be outside, but when she is ready to sit, she looks for me.

She loves her mom too! It's funny when we're all in the same room, and we call her just to see whom she chooses. I never get tired of her love and attention.

Bonnie is the sweetest baby ever. Her mom just got married in October, and Bonnie stood at the front, next to her mom's fiancé. No one encouraged her to go; she just somehow knew it was a special day, and her place was with her family. That's Bonnie, our special girl.

Bonnie isn't the only Aussie who uses her paws to show affection. Our next Aussie's trick is to turn herself into an airline pillow.

An Aussie? Or An Airline Pillow?

Loren Taylor tells us about her loving dog, Sydney, who used to lie behind her on the sofa like a cat.

Sydney was truly my girl, and I knew it the moment I saw her on Petfinder. Even from the beginning, when I adopted her at three months old, she didn't need a leash. She always kept an eye on where I was. If I called her, she would come right back to me, as long as the ground didn't smell too good or food wasn't involved. (You have to remember that she was an Aussie, and they can be stubborn.)

Sydney had to sit next to me in the front seat whenever we traveled; riding in the back with her five brothers and sisters didn't work for her. She was a person, not a dog. If I left a room, she would follow me. Also, she would stay in bed with me as long as I did. She didn't care if we slept in or got up early: she just wasn't moving until I moved.

Photo Courtesy of
Loren Taylor

My favorite Velcro characteristic of Sydney's was that she used to sit on top of the back cushions of the couch and wrap herself around me like a cat. She would just curl up on the cushion behind my neck. It was like I had one of those airplane pillows, but one that was cute and snuggly.

I didn't train her to do it. She just did it on her own, starting when she was probably about four or five months old. Sydney decided the linoleum floor was lava, and she wouldn't walk on it to get to the back door to go outside. I had to carry her out for about a month. But the living room was carpet, and apparently safe. So, after zooming around the room, she'd pop up onto the couch and wrap herself around me. She only stopped when we moved in with my husband, Dan. Sydney would sit on the back of the couch between us. She loved my Husband Dan. Sydney was my girl from the moment we met, and she loved him too.

Up until a couple of days before she passed at age 14, she was still trotting around the yard and jumping on the couch. I lost her to natural causes in 2018. I still really miss her.

Sydney knew how to make her mom feel comfortable and loved, as did our next Aussie, who actively hugged her parents whenever they were feeling down.

Nothing's Better Than an Aussie Hug

Jeff Hutchinson tells us about Kayde, his first Australian Shepherd, who taught herself how to hug her parents.

We are a big Aussie family. Each of our Aussies has been incredibly intelligent, and really, they are the best dogs. We are on our fourth Aussie, but we got our first one, Kayde, in 1985. She was a special dog. She was highly affectionate (and Velcro-like) with my wife and me. Whenever I came home from work, she would jump up to lick me on the nose.

She was really possessive of my wife and me, and she wasn't good with strangers. We realized Kayde didn't get enough socialization as a pup, and we've worked with all of our Aussies since then to make sure they're good with strangers. Though we were a little nervous about having kids, she loved our boys from the start.

Kayde was so intuitive and affectionate. Once when my wife was at work and I was at home alone, I had a bad fall and couldn't get up right away. Kayde just sat beside me and licked my face until I was able to stand.

The most memorable thing about Kayde was that she taught herself how to hug us. I don't mean that we would hug her. She hugged us. The first time it happened, I got on my knees and said, "Give me a

Photo Courtesy of Jeff Hutchinson

hug." She immediately jumped up and put both of her paws on each side of my neck. When I put my arms around her, she used her paws to pull me closer for a hug. I didn't train her to do that; she just knew that's what I was asking for.

Kayde would regularly hug my wife Sheryl and me, but no one else—not even our kids. We could ask her for a hug, and she would give it to us, but a lot of times, if she knew something wasn't right, and we were on our knees, she would just come over and hug us without being prompted.

One time I was having a bad day. I can't remember what I was upset about, but I knelt down to do something on the floor. Kayde came right over, pulled me in, and hugged me. It's been a long time since she passed away, but I will never forget her hugs.

★ ★ ★

If you have an Australian Shepherd, chances are you will never be alone again. Aussies just have a bond with their owners that is both sweet, affectionate, and sometimes a little too much. That is especially true if you are trying to get a turkey to the table or find your dog wrapped around your neck as you watch your favorite TV show.

However, this behavior may become troublesome if you don't rein it in early. If your dog gets underfoot too much or pushes children around, you'll need to send signals to your pet that this is not okay. For example, your dog may begin nipping or barking at a person's feet as they gear up for herding. Simply say 'no' firmly and walk away without making your dog cower. After a few repetitions, they will get the message and you can continue having a loving relationship without getting smothered.

What we've learned from these owners is that the fact that an Aussie is glued to your side (or your feet) isn't a bad thing. It's endearing, and part of what makes Aussies so incredibly lovable.

Chapter 3:

High-Energy Cyclones Of Playfulness

Australian Shepherds are originally bred to work, so they require plenty of exercise for body and mind to keep them engaged and happy. If they're not given a job, they will create one.

Just like most humans, they want their day to be filled with activities that keep their minds and bodies active. While some dogs like to lie in the sun and relax, Aussies will be looking out the window or scanning the horizon for something to keep them entertained. Once they see a chance to play a game or solve a problem, they are on it. And they will not stop.

What's it like to have an energetic Aussie? Let's hear from some owners.

Each Moment is an Opportunity for Play

Evie Hanson describes how challenging working from home can be with her energetic Aussie, Aristotle.

Aristotle is two years old and is the sweetest boy. He thinks he's a lapdog and gets jealous very easily. He always wants to be near us in case we go along for a ride or walk. As long as he's with us, he's happy as can be!

Aristotle is VERY playful. While I love his energy, it has been challenging during the pandemic. For the first time, he has had us both home, and he now wants to play fetch or tug-of-war while we are working.

*Photo Courtesy of
Evie Hanson*

No matter how many walks or drives we take or games we play, I don't think he'll ever tire.

Before the pandemic, he went to the dog park more often, so he could work off a lot of his energy there. Now that we're home all of the time, Aristotle's mood changes if one of us leaves the house or if he's alone. If we both leave the house, he is very clingy and anxious the first five minutes after we get back. Though there are fewer options for getting him out and about lately, we go on walks, visit doggy daycare to meet new friends (both dog and human), play fetch, or go on rides.

While having an energetic dog is tiring, it's a lot of fun! Trying to find different ways to help Aristotle work off his energy has been a journey in itself. We've looked into getting him a herding ball, different fetching toys, and other ways to calm him down. So far, though, the only thing that keeps him really happy is being around us.

Aristotle truly is such a blessing to our family. He always wants to comfort us when we're sad and show us love whenever he can. I couldn't have asked for a better dog, and he is the best paw friend a girl could ask for.

While Aristotle seems to want his owners around to burn off his boundless energy, some Aussies create their own games to stay busy.

It's a Ball All Day

Jeff Hutchinson tells us about Rio, his Aussie who is so full of energy, she has invented games to keep herself occupied all day.

I've had four Aussies, and they all have had boundless energy, especially as puppies. More so than other dogs. I think it's because of their hunting instinct and their need to herd. Without a sense of purpose, they can get bored easily and become destructive. (One of our Aussies once chewed the corner of our couch when she was restless.) In the absence of livestock, play becomes a Shepherd's job.

Photo Courtesy of
Jeff Hutchinson

Our Aussie, Rio, is three years old now. When she gets up in the morning, the first thing she does—even before we take her out to pee—is find her ball. She'll wake us up around five o'clock every morning, and you'd think the first thing she would want to do is be let outside. But instead she races to the living room to find where she left her ball the night before.

And then it's "ball" all day. Rio has invented a lot of games. She'll drop the ball on the linoleum floor in the kitchen and wait for it to bounce back so she can catch it. Over and over again, she'll play that game until she misses. Then she'll bring the ball to us in the living room and trick us into playing somehow.

She'll put the ball on the coffee table for my wife, and the two of them will play a little table ball. My wife will bounce the ball on the table for her, and Rio will catch it. When Rio gets tired of this game, she usually gets me to play with her next. I'll follow her into the other room and throw the ball so she has a longer way to run down the hallway. It's like she's herding the ball—and us—all day.

Aussies like to remind you that they're in charge—not you. Rio now has a new game where sometimes she barks at me if I'm sitting in the recliner. The first time she did it, I had no idea why, but my wife said she thought I needed to put the footrest up. So, I did, and Rio hopped on the chair with me and began nibbling my feet. Now she'll continue playfully biting my toes until I swing my feet up onto the windowsill right next to the chair. Then I'm safe, and the nibbling game is finished.

It's play all day for Rio. Aussies are workaholics, and that play gives them a sense of purpose.

Rio isn't the only dog who invents her own games to burn off her energy. Our next Aussie has created her own obstacle course and game of tag with her siblings.

Outdoor Furniture = An Aussie's Obstacle Course

Loren Taylor tells us about Harley, her Aussie, who has so much energy, she created her own obstacle course out of the outdoor furniture.

Harley is a 32-pound black tri-Aussie that we rescued from Australian Shepherds Furever when she was about four months old. Pretty much from day one, Harley started turning our outdoor furniture into an obstacle course—jumping on the outside coffee table, pool table, and bar chairs. It all started a couple of weeks after we got her. She loves to run around the yard doing zoomies, then she would pop up straight in the air with perfect precision and land on the outdoor coffee table or lounge chair.

We feed the pups in a room that has a pool table, couch, TV, and access to the backyard. (We call it the "mog" room: half man cave,

Photo Courtesy of Loren Taylor

half dog room.) My husband, Dan, uses the pool table to get the dogs' food ready. Once, Harley was so excited for dinnertime, she jumped straight up and landed on the table. We also have a bar-height chair in the mog room. Without warning, she will pop up there and wait for you to pet her.

Every day, she runs around and jumps on the outside coffee table, chaise lounge, couch, and barstool. I think the coffee table outside is now her home base. When Loki (our GSD) is chasing her, Harley will pop up on the coffee table, and all chasing stops for a breather. Then off they go again!

Although most of her chasing and game-playing is on the outdoor furniture, Harley loves the couch and the bed. She and Loki think our bed is the perfect spot to play and wrestle.

Photo Courtesy of Loren Taylor

Harley is amazing. I have seen her turn so quickly that Loki can't keep up with her. I have seen her spin and jump over Loki so she can't catch her. (Loki is fast too.) She also likes to do swimmers' turns on my couch. I never taught her that trick—it's a flyball sport move where Harley will jump onto one end of the couch with both her front paws and turn 180 degrees in midair, skillfully launching herself off the couch with her back feet.

It is play, play, play, play, all the time. While we're watching TV, and all the other pups are lying around, we have to throw Harley's toys. If one of us ignores the toy she placed so nicely on our lap, she will jump on us to get our attention. The cutest trick she does is that if she wants you to launch the toy, and she doesn't hand it to you or place it in your lap (meaning it's still on the floor), you tell her you can't reach it, and she will then pick the toy up and put it directly in your hand.

Harley's zoomies seem pretty tame compared to an Aussie who runs around with farm and wild animals every chance he gets.

Fleck the Farm Runner

Ashlee Rutherford introduces us to Fleck, an Aussie who is always running around the farm, making friends with animals, and herding deer.

My nine-year-old Blue Merle Australian Shepherd, Fleck, is energetic, playful, and loving. He is always running around the farm doing something. He herds the cats, tries to herd the chickens through their fence, and you can even hear him running with the coyotes.

Fleck and Buddy the horse were best friends. They loved each other. Fleck would run to the fence and bark for Buddy if he didn't see him in the pasture, and Buddy would always come running to meet him. Sometimes if Fleck didn't come to the pasture, Buddy would whinny and neigh, then Fleck would run to him. After they greeted each other, Fleck would slip into the pasture and run with Buddy. You could look outside and see the two of them running through the whole pasture together.

When I was 18, I moved in with my grandfather and brought Fleck with me. He missed being on the farm, but my dad had sold Buddy, so I thought Fleck might be happier where he couldn't smell where his friend had been.

When we moved in with my grandfather, it was a big change for Fleck, coming from a farm to a smaller property. At first, he just stayed around the house and lost a little weight, but soon he realized he could follow my grandfather around on his Kawasaki Mule. He fell in love with everyone that lived in the area. You could find him running up and down the gravel driveway to each of my grandfather's brothers and sister to get a treat.

Eventually, I had to move Fleck back to the farm, but he didn't have Buddy around anymore, so he had to make new friends with the local deer population. Every night, around the same time, you could hear Fleck out in the forest surrounding the farm, barking and yipping. Then you would see two or three deer come bounding out at full speed, and Fleck would be right there with them. Now, he's getting older and isn't quite as spry and energetic as he used to be, but when something trespasses on his territory, you can bet he will still chase it off.

Fleck is not alone; other farm Aussies use their boundless energy to herd anything they can, including alpacas.

Photo Courtesy of Ashlee Rutherford

From Fat Boy to Hunk

Cindy Fronk tells us the story of Pierce, whose endless activities on the farm transformed him from an overweight Aussie into a trim and energetic farmhand.

We got Hawkeye Pierce, a blue-eyed Blue Merle slightly younger than a year old, from a reputable Aussie breeder here in Colorado who took the dog back after his original buyer/owner said Pierce was dumb and couldn't learn. After the breeder evaluated Pierce for several weeks, she told us that "he was one of the smartest pups she had ever raised...perhaps too smart for his original owner."

Pierce was rather chunky, and we affectionately nicknamed him "Fat Boy." Since we had another young Aussie, "Waltzing Matilda" (a.k.a. "Tilly"), we already understood the high activity level this breed exhibits, along with Aussies' astounding intellect and their strong need for a "job." We were hoping that the two dogs would keep each other company (and out of mischief) until we moved to the country.

It was obvious from the get-go that Tilly was the boss, and Pierce was supposed to follow her lead. If he ever forgot, Tilly would remind him that she was the alpha dog (she ate and drank first, went out the door first, was petted by visitors first, etc.). Tilly growled/grumbled/snapped at Pierce and inserted herself into the "prime" position. Pierce was such a laid-back, silly, goofy guy that he could usually defuse one of Tilly's tense etiquette lessons by flopping down on his back and licking Tilly's face. She never stayed mad at him for long. Pierce was a true pleaser, whether he was doing his best for people or making friends with another dog. He never met anyone he didn't like (except squirrels).

In June, we moved out to the ranch, and Pierce was more enamored with our pond than he was with our 20 enclosed acres. It became a frequent ritual for both dogs to roll in the horse poop, go swimming in the pond, then get hosed off and shampooed before they were allowed back into the house. Swimming in the pond was heaven for the dogs.

Pierce could finally run off his energy and keep our pastures safe from all the birds, squirrels, and bunnies. He would run all day, twirl in circles, and play up and down the fence lines with our horses. Before snow fell that first winter, Pierce the Fat Boy had lost close to 10 pounds and was buff and fit! His physical transformation was amazing. Soon we had to start calling him "Hunk."

We knew Pierce was happy, but we didn't want him to die of a heart attack from all his exercise. Pierce would literally spend hours each day running. Meanwhile, Tilly would lie in the shade and grumble at him when he looked like he was having too much fun with all his jumping and twirling in the air. Playing and interacting with the horses became Pierce's daily job.

We quickly learned, though, that Aussies are absolutely the wrong kind of dog to have around alpacas. Aussies naturally want to herd everything—the neighbor's cows, our horses, people, poultry, and the alpacas! However, alpacas herd about as well as cats: they don't. So, we set about training the dogs to never go into the paddocks or pastures with the alpacas. They totally understood that they could chase up and down fence lines with the horses, but they were not allowed to harass or try to herd the alpacas!

After a couple of weeks, we noticed that Tilly and Pierce would actually turn their heads and not even make eye contact with the alpacas. In over a dozen years of having both Aussies and alpacas together on the ranch, we never had one unpleasant incident.

Tilly passed away at about 15 years old, and Pierce lived until almost 17. He became like a doddery old man with poor mobility, worse vision, and limited hearing, but he remained our sweet and silly boy right up until the end.

As we've learned, Australian Shepherds have a seemingly endless amount of energy. They will play, run, and create games for themselves. Occasionally, they will tire out their humans or challenge their owners with their endless need for playtime and walks.

Those lucky Aussies that get to run around on farms will use their boundless energy to befriend and herd whatever animals they might find. If your pet doesn't have a large acreage to blow off steam, it's best to make plans and games to keep them moving so they don't turn that energy into destructive behavior. Invest in Frisbees or even a flyball machine so they can hit a lever and launch a ball to retrieve. If you catch them chewing or ripping up a household item, redirect their energy to a toy or a different activity so they learn what is right and what is not.

Owners who understand their Aussies' highly energetic nature and give them the freedom both to play and to work are rewarded with happy, helpful, and loving pups.

Chapter 4:
Hard-Working Allies

Australian Shepherds like to have a job. That's why they're really good at tasks like herding animals on farms, or search and rescue. Because Aussies are also extremely sensitive to their owners' needs, they can make great emotional support dogs or mobility assist dogs, as we'll hear from a couple of owners.

Australian Shepherds are eager to please their humans. They can be an incredible asset, but they also might get into a bit of trouble if they don't have work to do.

As their keepers, it's up to their owner to help them find constructive ways for them to help with our daily tasks. This may be as simple as accompanying them on walks or hikes or playing with other pets and members of the family. As you will see in this chapter, they read human cues well to see if they are doing a good job or not. They are up to any job, whether it is physical work or emotional support.

Penny the Mind-Reader

Pamela Long tells us about her Aussie, Penny, a dog who works alongside her at the farm, anticipating her every move.

I adopted Penny in January 2018 after seeing her photo on Facebook. She was a few years old at that point, and I was concerned that she wouldn't bond with me. But I didn't need to worry.

From day one, Penny has never strayed more than a few feet from my side. She amazes me. We live in a remote rural area in southeastern Arizona. There are numerous distractions to lure a curious dog into venturing off on her own. Horses, dogs, cats, pack rats and mice, many species of snakes (including rattlesnakes), lizards, Gila monsters, coyotes, bobcats, mountain lions, javelina, coatimundi, badgers, deer, and other critters, including bears, are abundant. No problem. Penny stays close, clearly seeing herself as my protector.

As I drive my Gator, Penny rides in the seat beside me, usually with her paw resting on my leg or my arm. I make several stops at different

Photo Courtesy of Pamela Long

pastures to throw hay, feed, grain, and fill water tanks. Penny stays mostly on her seat in the Gator, patiently watching and waiting. She rarely exits the vehicle unless I wander out of her sight or she perceives a threat, such as advancing critters or humans. Replenishing our two wildlife water stations signals the end of chores. Penny knows our last stop, and she usually exits the Gator and runs up the hill to the barn.

Penny is an incredibly smart dog who anticipates my every move. Or maybe she reads my mind. When I scoop horse manure, she knows it's her time to explore nearby, so she gets out of her seat. When I set down the manure fork, she heads back to the Gator. I am certain she studies my mannerisms, watches which keys I grab, observes my gestures, and knows my routines.

Penny turns herself inside out trying to please me. If I tell her, "No," one time, that's it. She never repeats that behavior again. For instance, when I feed the cats in the barn, it's okay for Penny to clean up the leftover canned food since it draws flies and makes a mess. However, I once told her, "No," when she started eating the cats' dry food. I swear now she would starve to death before she would ever touch it again.

Very infrequently, I do morning chores with my truck rather than the Gator. Somehow Penny knows and automatically heads for the different vehicle.

I board dogs, and occasionally we have more visiting dogs than we have kennels. As a result, sometimes Penny is relegated to the kitchen or my bedroom. She seems to automatically know when there is a change and where she is supposed to go. She is there waiting for me to open the door or gate before I even get there.

Penny is always by my side, and always ready to work with me and for me.

Penny is a great example of how helpful an Australian Shepherd can be on a farm. But what about an Aussie that just wants to make your everyday life easier?

An Aussie So Obedient, She Tinkles On Demand

Christa Reynolds tells us about Bella, an Aussie so obedient and eager to please, that she will go to the bathroom immediately if she receives the command.

Bella is a Blue Merle Aussie. She is 11 years old and is extremely well-trained. When she was a puppy, we did a two-week immersion training for her, but otherwise, she's just automatically picked up little tricks and habits along the way that have made our lives easier. She is the fastest ball fetcher and runner I have ever seen, and she is a Frisbee dog, through and through.

Bella is an amazing listener, and she will do whatever you want—she just wants to know when and how. She loves to please us so much

Photo Courtesy of
Christa Reynolds

that she will tinkle on demand. Now, when I say, "on demand," I don't mean she goes within a few blocks of when you ask her to. I mean it's immediate. We give her the command "go tee," and within three or four steps of when you say those words, she will squat wherever she is and do her business. There is no sniffing, no picking out a place, no back and forth—she just does it.

I remember one time when we were on a road trip. We'd gotten out of our car, and we were in a concrete parking lot. There was no grass for at least 30 feet. There was a tree a little bit closer, but not much. I said, "Bella, go tee," and she just squatted on the concrete and tinkled on demand. I couldn't believe it. I thought she'd at least wait until we got to a tree!

That's my Bella. Always eager to please and will do whatever you ask her to.

Bella isn't the only Australian Shepherd who is eager to please. Our next Aussie takes her desire to be helpful to her mom to a whole new level.

The Aussie Peacekeeper

Julie Reese tells us about Zoie, an Aussie who is so keen to work for her mom's happiness that she will duck her head in shame if anyone in her family does something wrong.

Zoie has always been very expressive with all her emotions since the moment I got her at about eight months of age. Her tail is the indicator of her happiness! It spins like a helicopter rotor when she is pleased with anything. You just know when Zoie is happy: her eyes sparkle, her ears are all perked up, and she smiles. She also has happy growls and "ruffs."

She is very obedient. She will nudge her way under my hand to get my attention, then walk over to what she wants to get my okay to have it.

Zoie is so intent on pleasing me that she gets a totally disgusted look on her face when she makes a mistake. The first time she made this face was when she had an accident in my house. She and I were not on the same page yet for a schedule since she had been an outside dog. Poor girl, she was humiliated! If she could have turned red, I think she would have. I let her know it was okay, and we went to the backyard. From there on out, she knew to come to me when she needed to go.

She will make that same face whenever anyone gets a stern talking-to, even when I'm talking to the cat! (I wonder if before I got her, the man who owned her yelled a lot, because she does not like a raised or harsh voice.) Even when my kids were in high school, and I'd holler for them to bring me something, Zoie would duck her head

Photo Courtesy of
Julie Reese

and make her disgusted face. I try not to yell in front of her anymore because she takes on all the world's mistakes.

Luckily, I can now give her what my girls call my "mom look," and Zoie will stop what she is doing, come to my side, and duck her head. She rarely makes mistakes anymore, but she's a follower of our other dog, Tonks, who is naughty!

Tonks is a rescue who was born to a Golden Retriever mom and a mystery dad. She gets in trouble all the time! Zoie knows when I am mad at Tonks, and she will slink away with her head down, stub of a tail tucked, and that look of disgust on her face.

However, when Tonks gets the gate open, Zoie is gone with her on an adventure! In our small town, everyone knows my girls and will point me in the direction they have gone. Usually they are up the hill, swimming in the neighborhood pond. They see me driving up, and Zoie will duck her head and grimace and slink into the back seat while Tonks will grin, happily grumble, and barrel into the car.

On the drive home, I "yell" at Tonks, and Tonks thinks all is good in her world. (I swear she ignores me.) Meanwhile Zoie will stare out the side window so she doesn't have to make eye contact of any kind. When we get home, Zoie slinks onto her pillow while Tonks bounces around me to see if I will "let" her do something else fun! I think after five years of Tonks, Zoie and I have decided we cannot discipline her because she just doesn't care and doesn't listen.

Zoie's distaste for her sister's disobedience is a beautiful expression of an Aussie who loves to work for her mom's happiness, a lot like our next Aussie.

As Long as Chloe is Around, Everything is Okay

Jacklyn Thymian tells us about Chloe, her PTSD service dog, who lives for her owner's happiness.

Chloe was born April 25, 2016. She is very free-spirited and loves to run and play, but she also loves to be near me and is very loyal. She lives for when I pull out my treat bag and teach her new things. She can learn a new trick in one or two sessions.

Chloe has multiple trick dog titles and agility titles. She loves to throw her squeaky tennis ball up in the air and catch it just for fun. She also will do silly things just to hear me laugh.

She also has another important job. Chloe is my post-traumatic stress disorder (PTSD) service dog. When I'm having a really rough day, she knows it and never leaves my side. She performs deep pressure therapy by lying on me and putting her body weight on my lap. This helps ground me and bring me back from flashbacks. It also helps calm and relax me. (This is similar to a weighted blanket for people with autism.)

Chloe loves her squeaky tennis ball, and just the other day, when I was having an off day, she performed deep pressure therapy while holding onto her squeaky tennis ball. She also wakes me up from night terrors (more severe versions of nightmares), which is immensely helpful. Last month, when I had a bad night terror, she brought her ball to me after she woke me up.

When I'm sad, Chloe will come put her head in my lap and look up at me with her sweet eyes. It just makes me feel better about everything, knowing that Chloe cares.

Chloe works to give her owner physical and emotional support. Our next Australian Shepherd helps her owner with mobility challenges.

Photo Courtesy of
Jacklyn Thymian

SERVICE DOG

Kayla, the Mobility-Assist Aussie

Renee Marshall introduces us to Kayla, an Aussie who intuitively knows how to care for her and serves as a mobility-assist dog now that Renee has developed hip problems.

Kayla is not my first Aussie, and I initially adopted her as a pet. I have had her since she was three months old.

She was about five years old when I developed a degenerative hip problem. I had some experience as a pet trainer and was able to teach her to do some things for me. She learned to "brace" and help me up when I fall. She would help me up if I sat on a piece of furniture that didn't have arms; she would lie across the chair or couch so I could push up on her to stand up.

As my disability progressed, she just knew what I needed. One time, when I was leaning over to pick something up, she stood next to me so I could hold onto her for stability. That's not something I taught her.

I was able to get her registered with Service Dogs of America after I explained to them what she does for me. She is now considered a mobility-assist dog.

Kayla is also certified as an emotional support dog. I worked with the

Photo Courtesy of Renee Marshall

elderly in nursing homes, so she went to work there with me as a therapy dog. She loved the residents, and they loved her. One employee was afraid of dogs, so much so that when someone else's small dog came running into our office, this lady screamed and jumped up on her desk. But after being around Kayla for a while, she learned that

Kayla was mellow, obedient, and sweet. Although she never wanted to get too close to my dog, the woman eventually felt comfortable allowing and even encouraging her three-year-old daughter to pet Kayla.

One night before bed, I somehow lost my balance, fell, and hit my head on the dresser. There was a lot of blood running down my face, even though it wasn't a big cut. Kayla was right by my side, trying to comfort me and make sure I was okay. We both settled in for the night. But when I got up for potty breaks during the night, I noticed that she was sitting up, alert, and watching me. This was not a normal night for her; she usually is asleep.

Kayla helps me in so many ways. I am very thankful to have her.

***

Aussies are capable herding dogs, gifted with both immense skill and instincts. They can also excel in obedience and agility.

Those skills can be translated to helping their humans in a variety of other ways. They can help out on the farm or tinkle on command to make their owners' lives easier. As you train your dog, think about the ways you reinforce how they help you and reward them for a job well-done. It is so easy, with humans or pets, to just take small acts of kindness for granted. However, a quick thank-you message makes your pet realize how much you appreciate their help. You can do this with a little piece of kibble but an affectionate ear rub will be golden to your dog as well.

Australian Shepherds are talented at more than pleasing their owners and performing chores. They are also intuitive, sensitive, and caring animals that can serve their owners in providing the most meaningful physical and emotional support, which is why they are often used as therapy dogs.

Whatever jobs they are given, Aussies are ready to step up to the task and help their owners get the work done.

Chapter 5:

Devoted Family Members

A consistent trait among Australian Shepherds is that they are incredibly devoted to one human. The only trouble is, Aussies do the choosing of the particular person to whom they're loyal—not you.

This devotion might be shown in a variety of ways. Some Aussies seem to forget they have other people in the household when their main person is around; others might even use that devotion to try to protect their number one from spouses and other family members. Dogs are so transparent that they cannot keep any secrets, including the person they have made their favorite. They cling to them, wag their tails more vigorously for them, and sit by a window or door and wait for them for hours. Yes, you will always know where you stand with your Aussie.

Australian Shepherds' allegiance is a characteristic that owners adore about them, even if it might get the dogs into trouble from time to time.

He Chose My Husband

Katrina Bartoli shares a common story among Aussie owners: "We thought he was going to be my dog, but it turns out he loves my husband more."

Gus was born on Jan. 28, 2020. We adopted him from an Amish puppy mill that was planning to take him to the pound because they thought he was too timid. We brought Gus home when he was 10 weeks old. I wish I had gotten him sooner so that his beginning weeks would have been more positive. He's outgoing with the family, but a little shy around strangers until he knows you.

We knew from the beginning that he would need a job in order to keep his busy mind out of trouble. He is a farm dog: he loves running and is a zoomer; if he isn't doing a task at 110 miles per hour, then he isn't doing it at all.

When we got him, I thought Gus would be my dog. It turns out that he loves my husband best instead. I work from home, and Gus is usually under the desk, at my feet, all day. But when my husband gets home from work, Gus is with him from the time he hits the front door until he sits down. Then it's a matter of keeping Gus out of my husband's lap.

My husband likes Mike and Ikes candies and Swedish fish, and so does Gus. Anytime he hears my husband rattle the bag, Gus starts whimpering and whining to get a treat. If allowed, he will practically lick the skin off my husband's face and hands. But Gus has never licked me even once. And I don't think it has anything to do with the candy.

Recently, my husband was outside, putting Christmas lights on the house. Once he climbed the ladder, Gus was determined to also get up on the roof. I eventually had to put him in his crate.

Whenever my husband is home, Gus will always be wherever his favorite human is. With me, he couldn't care less. And if Gus isn't with my husband, then he's with our youngest, Nicholas, who's eight years old. I know the pecking order of Gus's love, and I'm at the bottom!

Gus shows his affection and devotion for his dad by following him around nonstop. Our next devoted Aussie might leave her mama's side, but never for long.

A Devoted Diva

Christa Reynolds tells us about her stubborn girl, Indie, who shows her devotion by never straying too far from her on walks.

My younger Aussie, Indie, has only ever had me as her caretaker. Her personality is such that she is a stubborn diva. She's the type of dog who will catch a Frisbee and let it drop in front of her, just so that you have to come and get it to throw it to her again.

But stubborn or not, Indie is devoted to me. She hikes a lot with our other dogs and us. We'll go on a forest walk that spans more than 40 acres and has deer, bears, and a lot of other distractions. Indie will maybe get 50 yards ahead, but no more. Once she went 100 yards while the dogs were all chasing a deer, but she's never gone any further than that. And she always looks back to see where I am.

Indie's sister, Bella, is also an Aussie, but Bella will go to just about anyone and forget about me while we're on walks. Indie, on the other hand, is a mama's girl. If we go on a walk for only one mile, Indie will have covered 15 miles because she constantly circles back to wait for me.

Indie's devotion is so strong that she gets separation anxiety whenever I'm away from her. I was away for a few days recently, and she's been giving me the cold shoulder ever since I got home. It's like she is saying, "Mom, you're not allowed to leave without me."

Indie acts like she'd prefer to be a single-dog family. She'll wrestle with the other dogs and clean their ears. But she is 100 percent a mama's girl and would love to have me all to herself. I love how devoted she is to me.

Indie's devotion (and corresponding separation anxiety) is taken to the next level by Ruger, who will do anything to keep his owner all to himself.

Photo Courtesy of
Christa Reynolds

So Devoted, He Resorts to Thievery

Pam VonPressantin describes her Aussie, Ruger, who is so devoted to her that he steals her shoes so she can't leave the house without him.

I have a four-year-old black tri-Australian Shepherd named Ruger. He is a show dog; he has his AKC Grand Champion and ASCA Championships. My breeder shows him, so Ruger lives with me and travels with her.

Ruger is a fun, loving dog. He loves to give hugs to total strangers, but he's extremely attached to me. He enjoys going places and delights in playing, yet he will come and tell me what the other dogs are doing outside if they are being naughty.

He is devoted to me and will follow me around throughout the day. Even if I sit down, get back up again, and go back to where I came from because I've forgotten something, he will still follow me, but he'll puff out his lips and give me a look like, "Really? Again?"

I brought him home when he was nine weeks old, and about the third week after we got him, I noticed he had taken off with a shoe when it was time for me to go to work. He would normally go with me if we went anywhere. So when I put my work bag next to the door, he knew

Photo Courtesy of Pam VonPressentin

that I was leaving, while he had to stay home. He didn't like that idea.

At first, I thought I had misplaced my shoe. Finally, I decided I had to get ready to leave and got out another pair of boots. When I went outside to

Photo Courtesy of Pam VonPressentin

bring Ruger into the crate, I found him and my boot by the fence. I picked up the boot, and Ruger jumped up to take it from me. Later, my slippers and other shoes ended up out there so often, it became a daily thing.

I even tried putting the work bag in the car the night before to trick him, but he still knew. Then he would just take several shoes (one from each pair) outside, even in the snow.

After about a year, we broke him of the habit. But because of the pandemic, now I've been home a lot more and not working. When I was getting ready to go to the grocery store the other day, I went to put on my shoes and noticed I only had one. When I went outside, sure enough, Ruger had moved one.

He also doesn't like me reading my Kindle because it means I can't pay attention to him, so he started taking the Kindle up to the hill in the backyard along with my reading glasses. He has broken two pairs of my prescription glasses, and he cracked the screen to the Kindle. If I read paper books, he would tear those to shreds! He does the same with my shoes and belongings.

Ruger doesn't do that kind of thing with anyone else, although he absolutely loves my grandchildren. He will lie on the floor with them to play or color or put puzzles together.

Ruger shows his devotion with a little mischief (and thievery). Our next Aussie's devotion leads to some inadvertent troublemaking.

Nothing Can Keep Her Away
(or Out of the Way)

Pamela Long describes her Aussie, Penny's, devotion, which keeps her by her side and inconveniently underfoot on the farm.

I am 75 and have had dogs all my life. But I tell people that having an Aussie is like having a dog for the very first time because each Aussie is so different. My 14-year-old Australian Shepherd, Jake, died in August, and I was lost without him. I saw Penny's picture on Facebook in December, and she looked like a female Jake. They thought she was three or four years old.

I applied to adopt Penny right away. It was so long before I heard from the rescue that I almost gave up hope. Then, finally, a woman phoned out of the blue and asked if Penny could come for a visit. "Sure thing," I replied. Penny's foster mom brought her to my place a day later, in January 2018.

To tell you the truth, I had almost given up on the notion of adopting another dog. I already had two dogs (a Boxer and a Boxer/Heeler mix), and they kept me busy. I also worried that Penny would not bond with me. There was no way in the world Jake would have ever bonded with anyone other than me because he moved in with me when he was just six weeks old. So, I had to wonder—at three or four years old, would Penny connect with me? She had lived in at least four places before she arrived at my home.

After her foster mom left, though, Penny immediately adopted me. For the first two weeks, Penny and I took walks every day with her on her leash. The third week, Penny begged to walk off-leash, and I reluctantly relented. I didn't need to worry. From day one, Penny never strayed more than a few feet from my side, even though there are a million distractions on the farm in the form of other animals and critters. She immediately bonded with me and established herself as my protector.

Penny sticks to me like glue. I swear she reads my mind when it comes to my movements or chores. What Penny doesn't know, however, is when to get out of the way. Since she loves to be so close to me, she is constantly underfoot. She does not move to avoid an approaching horse, nor does she get out of my way in the kitchen. She seems unaware that no two things can occupy the same space at the same time. Thus, once in a while, our horses and I will accidentally step on her.

One fateful day, Penny ran right in front of the Gator (our farm utility cart) as I was driving it up the hill to the barn after our last stop. She had pretty serious road rash and bruises on her stomach. Even worse, she broke a couple of bones in her foot as well as two toes. Penny had surgery to repair her foot, and I was stuck with a $7,300 vet bill. I'm just thankful she didn't run in front of the truck because it could have been a lot worse.

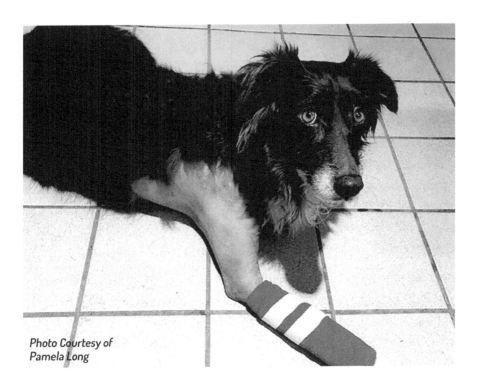

*Photo Courtesy of
Pamela Long*

During Penny's recovery, I stayed with her as much as possible. She and I spent the better part of our time together watching TV. Once a week for nearly four months, we drove 60 miles to Tucson so the vet could monitor her recovery then re-splint and rewrap her foot. Although Penny loves to ride in my truck with me and eagerly climbs in when she is given a chance, she also stressed a bit during those rides. I suspect the combination of her dread of vet visits and her fear of being left somewhere new rested uneasily on her mind.

She is fully healed now, and she now rides in the Gator during chores, just in case she decides to run in front of it again. The bottom line is that Penny is devoted to me, so much so that she sometimes gets into trouble. But I'm honored that she lives her life by my side.

Penny's devotion to her mom sometimes causes a little bit of trouble. Our next Australian Shepherd is equally obsessed with her mom and shows it in some hilarious (and socially inappropriate) ways.

We've Created a Giant Fuzzy Monster!

Mary Sanders tells us about how Juno protects her from every threat, even holding hands with or hugging her husband.

We had discussed getting a dog for about a year before Juno arrived. From day one, Juno was definitely our baby. My husband and I shared all the training, feeding, bathing, and everything. I could not handle the tiny shark teeth while playing, though, so my husband tended to get Juno a little more excitable, often encouraging her to bark and growl and go crazy with her toys. He would start off by cuddling her, then he'd go right into teasing and roughhousing.

I just wanted to pet Juno and snuggle her constantly. I hated crate training her because I wanted her next to me all the time. She tested us daily with her problem-solving skills and certainly kept us on our toes that first year. I read books and joined groups to learn as much as I could about her thinking and personality. I spent time watching her and working on various behaviors and, over time, began to truly connect with her.

The more I followed Juno around the house to make sure she wasn't getting into anything she shouldn't, the more she would follow me. I would peek around the corner to find her already staring in my direction. As soon as our eyes connected, she would jump up and come to me, wiggling with excitement. It would make my heart melt (and still does!), and she'd get some butt scratches and face smooches.

Juno was about two and a half when I was offered the option to work 100 percent from home. We lived in a safe little subdivision, but still on a side of Nashville that had a history of crime greater than most other areas. My husband wanted to make sure Juno could notify me of anything out of the ordinary, for times when I have on my headset for a conference call or webinar. He trained her to bark at any knocking and also whenever the front or back door would open.

My husband would tiptoe around the house and reward Juno when she barked, to train her to react to anyone who might make it inside the house. Even further, he would pretend to grab my arm as I yelled, to train Juno to bark ferociously should a possible intruder actually get close to me. The key, though, was that she was not allowed to bite. It was a completely verbal reaction on her part, and Juno still has varying volumes of barking that she understands for different situations.

Juno was already following me from room to room around the house, but after her training, she would actually "attach" to me and lie down with a back leg or her fuzzy butt touching my foot. She would immediately sit on my side of the couch when I got comfortable. She began to sleep next to me in bed at night. If I got up to use the bathroom, she followed. If I shut the door, she would whine, paw, and breathe heavily into the crack underneath. I would walk through the house and just stop, and she would run into the back of my legs. We often joke that Webster's Dictionary even put out a new edition with Juno's picture under "shadow"!

One Christmas, we were visiting family, and, as usual, everyone wanted to see Juno's newest tricks. She was playing with our nieces in the next room, and my husband yelled, "I'm going to get her!!!", and grabbed my arm. I screamed, and Juno came flying around the corner, barking like a rabid beast, with a rope toy in her mouth. She body-slammed into my husband, just about knocking him over, but not once letting go of her toy! She received a bunch of butt scratches and pets, and we assured her that she had saved her mama and was a good girl.

Shortly thereafter, the family (about 15 of us) gathered around in a big circle to join hands and say grace. Just as we heard "Dear Lord," my husband and I felt claws on our hands. Juno had both front feet pawing at our hands! We let go, and she sat down. We joined hands, and she pawed again! My husband gave her the visual command for "down," which she obeyed. We joined hands again, then felt her teeth! Not biting per se, but like puppy chewing and whining.

We both gave her the visual for "down" this time. She collapsed with a disgruntled, whiny growl, and it was extremely difficult to not burst out laughing in the middle of the prayer. We tried one more time to hold hands, and she started barking like a crime was being commit-ted! The entire room just about died laughing!

We ate dinner, opened gifts, and enjoyed everyone's company, but as everyone began saying their goodbyes, Juno began barking again. She'd stop, then bark again! My husband was getting a little irritated, then as I hugged my brother-in-law, Juno jumped at us! My hus-band and I hugged, and she jumped at us too. Every time I hugged someone, she would bark and jump at us. We had created a giant fuzzy monster!

Juno's obsession with me has been a tad annoying at inappropriate times over the years, but she only does what she has been trained to do. I certainly appreciate her protection and thankfully have never had to put it to the test. She is now just as protective over our toddler (her little brother).

Devotion from an Aussie can be seen as a display of love, affection, and enthusiasm for a particular person. They might show devotion to just one owner by staying by one person's side 24/7 and creating a bit of trouble by being in the way sometimes. Or they might create obstacles to their owners leaving.

Meanwhile, others might show their devotion by trying to protect their favorite person from an "attack" of affection from a family member. Rather than letting this behavior continue, owners need to make it clear that they make the rules and things don't get too far out of hand. While it may be cute for a puppy to nip to keep someone at bay, that is not a habit that you want to see carry forward into adulthood. Since they learn so quickly, a quick but consistent reminder is all it will take for your dog to get the message that while they can play favorites, they have to do so nicely.

Regardless of how they show it, Australian Shepherds' devotion to their owners is a sweet and loving trait that demonstrates their loyalty to those who care for them.

Chapter 6:
A Loyal Protector

As we have learned, Australian Shepherds are devoted to their owners and their properties. This goes hand in hand with our next trait, which is that they are undeniably protective of their owners. As they were bred to look after farm animals, they have a strong instinct to defend their humans.

Just think about the dangers the Aussies' ancestors have faced, such as large predators and livestock poachers. They become very attuned to the routines of a household or farm and become wary when new people or situations arise. If they think they sense danger, they will let their owners know and act to protect the people and animals in their lives.

Sometimes Australian Shepherds can be so alert to danger (or perceived danger) to their humans that they become household enforcers. They might even take on the role of a security guard, making sure everyone is safe in the home. And some Australian Shepherds might be such fierce protectors of their humans that they even save their lives.

A Puppy Protector

Katrina Bartoli tells us about her Aussie, Gus, and how, as a puppy, he was already ferociously guarding the house.

Our Australian Shepherd, Gus, is just about one year old. He is leery of strangers. Once he knows you, he is less shy, but it takes some time for him to warm up to new people.

Even though he's still a puppy, Gus has a big-dog bark and growl. He will protect the house, even if it means giving up his life. He is utterly devoted to us and our home.

Once we had a tree fall through our roof. We hired an Amish contractor to repair the damage. At some point, the contractor needed to come into our house, but 14-week-old Gus refused to let him in! He barked and growled so much we finally had to lock him in our laundry room to let the contractor in. The workers took almost five days to fix the house, and Gus was not happy about it, that's for sure.

When Gus was little, he would jump on my youngest child, Nicholas. One day, the dog even ripped his favorite shirt. Nicholas absolutely hated Gus after that point. But about six months ago, Nicholas was lying on the couch, and he shrieked because a stinkbug had landed on the couch. Gus went to investigate, then he found the bug and ate him. Now Nicholas will tell you that Gus is the best dog because he protected him from the stinkbug.

Gus also loves our barn cat, who comes up on the porch to eat his food. That stinky old tomcat can rub and lick Gus, and he loves it. They play tag around the tree in the yard. We often joke that Gus is a great watchdog, unless you're a cat—in which case a cat burglar could easily get into our house.

If it were up to Gus, no strangers would be allowed inside the house; if it were up to our next Aussie, no one would be allowed anywhere close to his property.

Beware of This Aussie

Jim Martin tells us about Buckey, the Aussie who chased away all intruders (and service people).

Our first Aussie was named Buckey. He was always watchful of strangers. He would stare at them with his golden eyes and his lip lifted on one side. Then he would follow their every move. If they came any closer, he would growl, just softly enough to warn them to stay away.

When he was about two years old, we called our electric company to have the light bulb changed on our power pole. Unfortunately for the lineman, he came a couple of days earlier than we expected him. He could see our Aussies in their run through the wire windows in the fence. At that point, they were barking, but nothing more. While our female Aussie just kept barking, Buckey cleared his six-foot chain-link fence and a six-foot cedar fence and trapped the lineman on the pole.

The lineman had to call his office, and Diane, my wife, had to come home to call Buckey off. The poor lineman was up on the pole for about 20 to 30 minutes. As soon as Diane arrived, Buckey went to her vehicle then ran back to the pole, looking so proud. He had to show her what he caught! Thankfully, the lineman was a dog guy, so he just laughed about it. He was a supervisor and hadn't climbed poles regularly for a while. He commented that he didn't know he could still climb that fast!

We figured out how Buckey got out. He quietly jumped on the doghouse, went over the gate, and came around the corner to the pole. (We changed the gate and moved the doghouse to avoid this escape route in the future.)

Several years later, my wife came home to find a blue sedan in our driveway with no one in sight. Our dogs were barking like crazy. My wife ran to the east side of the house by the backyard, and she saw an insurance adjuster coming toward her from the backyard fence. We had had hail in our area, and without notifying us, he had come by to inspect the damage.

Even though we had a "Beware of Dog" sign posted on the fence, the man climbed over the fence anyway (he admitted later that he ignored the sign). Once he saw Buckey, the guy immediately climbed back over the fence, with Buckey hot on his tail. Thankfully, our escape artist did not try to clear the fence this time. We locked the gate to the service yard and added more signs, then we warned all the service people that came to our house that we had a guard dog.

Buckey was an amazing watchdog; nothing got past his keen senses. No matter what, he protected his "pack." He was a strong alpha male, but he was very loyal and kind to us. With our family and those he knew well, he was very gentle; he even allowed our cats to cuddle with him. We were so lucky to have him in our family for 15-plus years.

While Buckey wouldn't let a stranger near his home, our next Aussie lets people in but makes sure to track their every move.

Photo Courtesy of Jim Martin

Chiro the Overseer

Loren Taylor describes how her Aussie, Chiro, would follow the exter-minator around the house to "help" him do his job.

Chiro, my very first Aussie, had quite the personality. For instance, when I would pick her up from boarding after returning from vacation, she would be so excited to see me. Her wiggling butt would go crazy! She would jump up and kiss me. But when we got home, and I would try to hug her more, she would just back up, bark, and talk to me: "Woo, woo, woo." Even though she had fun while she was away, she still had to let us know that she was mad at us for leaving her.

Photo Courtesy of
Loren Taylor

Chiro loved everyone, but she always made sure people who came to the house knew she was in charge. I was friends with our exterminator (we called him the "bug guy"). I always left my key so he could come in and spray. He would walk in, and Chiro and Ruby (my other Aussie) would meet him at the door. Ruby was not interested, so she would go back upstairs to lie on the bed.

Chiro was friendly and let the bug guy in. But really, she was saying, "Let me follow you around to make sure you are doing this right." If the bug guy had his head in a cabinet, Chiro's went in there too. I don't know if she was curious, she just wanted company, or she was making sure he didn't mess up the house. Either way, I found it hilarious that Chiro had to "help" the man do his job.

Chiro passed in 2011 due to natural causes. I really miss that pup. If Chiro could have talked, she would have had a lot to say.

Chiro let the exterminator off easily, compared to our next Aussie's relationship with the cable guy.

Fiercely Protective in Their Own Ways

Christa Reynolds has two Aussies, Bella and Indie, and each of them protects her in different ways.

I have two Aussies, Bella and Indie. Bella (the older one) is highly socialized, very easygoing, and she does well with tons of different people. My other Aussie, Indie, is another story.

Indie has mainly only been around me. She's been socialized, has gone hiking, and stays for long periods of time with friends while I'm away, but she suffers from severe separation anxiety. When I get back after being gone for a week, she immediately comes back to the door when I let her out, like, "Hey, don't leave me again."

Even though Bella and Indie couldn't be more different dogs, they are both protective of me. They just have a sixth sense about danger.

Photo Courtesy of Christa Reynolds

Bella (Left) and Indie (Right)

Bella will bark when people come to the house, and she will just sense when someone is not right. One time, a girlfriend and I were walking with Bella on the greenway in Georgia. It's a multiuse path in the woods—well-traveled, but still dangerous at times. We must have passed by at least 50 people that day, and Bella didn't react to anyone. But then a guy appeared on the trail who wasn't wearing workout gear, just street clothes. Bella must have sensed something off about him because she looked intensely at him and gave a low, threatening growl. The man didn't bother us.

Occasionally, there are times when Indie has felt threatened, or she has felt like I was being threatened, and she has just lowered her head and growled. It's not a vicious growl; it's a low message that "I'm watching you. If you come two steps forward, I am going to pounce."

Indie is fiercely protective of me. If some of my friends reach for me quickly, Indie will stand up and put her body between us. She's done that even with people we know really well.

Indie went nuts the other day on the cable guy—barking, growling, and becoming highly agitated. When she's in a state like that, she won't obey me at all. It's like her training goes out the window. You can't get through to her. She especially has a problem with people in uniform.

To let the cable guy inside the house, first I had to get Indie outside, which was no small feat. I was trying to get her to go out back, but she wasn't wearing her collar, and I couldn't grab her. At some point, she just turned around and put her butt in the air and her paws down on the ground and looked at me as if to ask, "Is this guy friend or foe?" When she did that, I said, "No, ma'am," and she immediately flopped on her back in her submissive posture.

Finally, I got her to go out without grabbing her. I just kept saying, "Indie, outside, outside," and walked her in that direction. She went from one window to the next, looking in the house and keeping an eye on us the entire time. The cable guy remarked, "Man, she's protective of you."

Bella is my calm, eager-to-please dog who will do anything immediately if given a voice or a sign command. No words have to be spoken. But Indie is my hot mess.

Indie and Bella are protective of their owner, and so is our next pair of Aussies.

They Are True Heroes

Kimberly Ward tells us a harrowing story about how her two Aussies saved her life during an attack by a pack of dogs on a remote hike in Alaska.

My two Aussies, Monk and Captain Jack, are nine years old. They've been with me since they were puppies. We've experienced a lot of different things; they've been by my side through tropical storms, a hurricane, a huge earthquake, blizzards, remote hiking adventures, two moose attacks, and injuries.

We live in Alaska, where we hike almost year-round. Unfortunately, not everyone follows leash laws. About three times a year, we encounter leash-less dogs that are aggressive.

Captain Jack and Monk have protected me a number of times. The most recent (and scariest) incident happened while we were hiking on a remote trail about 30 minutes from our house. The state park is 300,000 acres in size. Even though we usually follow a remote trail to try to avoid encounters with other dogs, mine are always on a leash.

That day we were having a beautiful hike. Coming back, I had veered off the trail to sit, have lunch, give my dogs some water, and take pictures. We were just about done when they whipped around behind me on the leash. I turned around and saw this huge dog coming right at me. It was a mix between a German Shepherd, a Great Dane, and a Husky. He was the biggest dog, with three more dogs following on his heels, but it was clear that he was the pack leader.

My dogs positioned themselves in-between the pack and me, block-
ing the aggressor. This dog towered over my dogs. He was waist
high, whereas my dogs are standard Australian Shepherds, coming
just above my knee. The pack leader had his eyes trained on me the
whole time, ignoring my dogs. I didn't want to let their leashes go.

Captain Jack and Monk worked as a team, stood their ground, and pre-
vented the pack leader from reaching me. They did everything right.

The other dogs in the pack were circling, yapping, and snapping—
supporting their leader. When the pack leader became frustrated
that my dogs wouldn't let him pass, he bit my submissive dog, Monk,

Photo Courtesy of
Kimberly Ward

Monk (Left) and Captain Jack (Right)

in the head. In response, Captain Jack jumped up and bit the pack leader, then Monk joined him and bit the dog on the head again.

It was messy, and quite a scuffle. While all of this was happening, the owners of this pack of dogs were way up the hill, running down it toward us. Even when the owners arrived and restrained the main dog, he was still lunging, barking and snapping at my dogs.

The owners got their dogs and left without even apologizing. I'm pretty even-keeled, but that day (and for a while after) I was really upset. I reported them to the park ranger, and he told me that we were lucky—my dogs had saved my life.

Thankfully, Australian Shepherds have so much fur you can stick your hand in their chest and lose your hand. Captain Jack and Monk were bitten quite a few times in that fight, but their dense fur probably saved them. They were both okay. On our way home, they got in the truck and lay on top of each other.

Their protective instinct, and the bond that we have, really kicked in. My Aussies probably saved my life and each other's. Incidentally, this was the third time they've protected me from aggressive dogs. They're true heroes!

***

The Australian Shepherd is many things, but being a steadfast protector of its owner and its pack is one of the breed's most admirable qualities. You will feel safe with this pack member by your side.

Aussies show their loyalty in different ways. Some Aussies are adorably protective of their owners as puppies, while others will clear fences to trap their prey, even if it is a service person called to the house. Some will just keep an eye on strangers, but sound the alarm.

In order for an Aussie to refine its radar of who is safe and who poses a danger, it helps to socialize a dog well as a puppy. By playing with other dogs and meeting more people, it will get more insights into when it encounters friendly and non-threatening mammals. Likewise, when it picks up on signals from dominant dogs, it will learn when it needs to step up and alert you to potential problems. That could save a lot of barking or embarrassing incidents if you need a repair in your home!

However they show it, and whether they demonstrate it in situations of perceived danger or actual danger, Aussies will do anything to stand up for the ones that they love.

Chapter 7:
Creatures Of Habit

Dogs need structure, and Australian Shepherds are no exception. It's important for Aussie owners to establish an orderly routine to let them know what to expect each day (food, exercise, and playtime) and when to expect it. If you don't create one, this type of dog will do it on their own.

It's helpful for them to understand what is going to happen when, including meals, walks and cuddle sessions. By having some order in their days, they will be more settled and focused, knowing not to bother the family during mealtimes or when to wake their owners up with a gentle nuzzle with a muzzle.

With consistent training and structure to their days, Australian Shepherds can be incredible companions and good helpers. With that said, sometimes Aussies might get a little too attached to their schedule. Some owners say that once they introduce a routine for their Australian Shepherds, there is no going back because the Aussies then take charge of their own daily patterns.

Maddie the Mathematician

Wendy Herzig tells us about her Aussie, Maddie's, morning routine, and how she's learned to count her morning treats.

Maddie Mae is a tri-colored black, brown, and white mini-Australian Shepherd. She's twelve years old and the best online purchase I ever made. We chose an Australian Shepherd because we found the breed to be a good mix of what both my husband and I wanted. My husband had a Border Collie when he was young; I had a Shetland Sheepdog. Since my husband is a scientist/mathematician and I am an over-analyzer, we delved into books and took online compatibility tests to find the breed that would "fit the bill."

My husband and I are both schoolteachers, so the majority of the year is quite regimented. The alarm heralds the day, and Maddie is taken out to "do her numbers" immediately.

Then we fill her food bowl, and she comes back into our bedroom for a little snack. She loves treats. However, she is extremely picky about what type. What dog doesn't like bacon-flavored treats? Ours.

If Maddie doesn't get her treat when she's supposed to, she will sit and look forlornly at the treat container. Should that not get our attention, she will start prancing to be noticed. As a last resort, she

Photo Courtesy of Wendy Herzig

will whimper. That always works, especially with my husband. She has him tied around her little paw.

Maddie Mae is also a mathematician. Perhaps she learned that from her human daddy? When we're leaving for the day, Maddie gets three little Milk-Bones thrown for her to retrieve. She doesn't start eating them until all three are in place. She stands at attention, watching as each bone hits the tile. After the first bone, she looks at the bone and stands. After the second bone, she looks at the bone, looks back at my husband, and stands. Finally, when the third bone makes its way to the floor, her treasure chest is complete. That's when she begins snacking.

If we are short a treat, we signal with open empty hands and say, "No more." She understands that to mean that only two are in the offering for the day. She accepts our paltry offering without whining and commences eating the two she did receive.

When this "counting" first happened, my husband and I just looked at each other and laughed. We wanted a smart dog, but Maddie definitely is more than we expected.

After our morning routine is finished, Maddie escorts us to the front door, where she sits and watches as we gather our items for the day. Once we bid her goodbye, she finds a place to continue her snooze. She is a lucky dog.

Needless to say, we adore our Maddie Mae. From the moment we gently pulled her from her travel crate, it has been a true love story. Licking is her love language. She is fun-loving, extremely attentive, fast-processing, and the guard of our castle. She is also our therapy dog, sensing when we are upset, tense, sad, etc., and always giving us more snuggles and licks when we need them!

Maddie Mae might be able to count, but our next Aussie can tell time.

He's in Charge of Our Schedule, Not Us

Linda Wilkoff tells us about their Aussie, Max, who keeps them on a schedule, even when they travel.

Max is six years old and really loves his family. He is reserved around strangers, but his smile gets big, and his eyes get brighter when our grandchildren come to play. Max also loves his tennis balls and his pig.

Photo Courtesy of Linda Wilkoff

We adopted Max in January 2015. He was rescued in West Virginia, and a friend of ours fostered him. We saw him and committed to him, sight unseen, then drove from Newfoundland, Canada, to bring him home. It was quite the drive, but it was worth it!

When we brought Max home, we introduced his schedule right away. Up at 6 a.m., other activities as designed, walk at 3 p.m., dinner at 5 p.m., play again at 7 p.m., and lastly bedtime at 8 p.m. But now he is in charge of that schedule, not us.

Max knows the time and his schedule. If we're off schedule for any reason, he comes and sits right in front of me. First, he just sits and looks at me. Then he will place his face on my leg. If I don't get the message, his last resort is to paw at me (with a smile).

The funny part is, even when we travel across time zones, he knows the time wherever we go. So, he keeps us on a schedule while we travel too.

Our next Aussie makes sure her owner follows her schedule to a tee.

No Time for Dishes

Lori Gladding tells us about Ame, who thinks her schedule must be followed precisely—no matter what else you might be doing at that moment.

My girl Amelia is a mini-Aussie, just a little over a year old. I call her Ame, but when I say "Amelia," she knows I mean business. When I first brought her home, she was three months old and scared of everything. She is still shy and intimidated by anyone other than me.

When I brought her home, I started her off with a schedule, and now she keeps me to it. At 7 a.m., we go out to the field behind our house to go to the bathroom. Around 10 or 11 a.m., we go out to pee. At 3:30 or 4:30 p.m., we go back out to the field to do our stuff. Between 5:30 and 8:30 p.m., Ame will ask me to go if she needs to. So far, in a

Photo Courtesy of Lori Gladding

year, she's only had two accidents since coming to live with me, and those were both in the kitchen.

She is very routine-oriented, so much so that she gets upset if her schedule is not followed to a tee. One of those times she had an accident, I was doing dishes and not paying attention to the hour. Unfortunately, it was Ame's time to go out. All of a sudden, I found her squatting behind my feet, deliberately peeing. I guess she couldn't wait a few minutes for me to finish my task!

Now that she is a little older, she will come to me and look me in the eye or bark if she needs to go. Regardless of her schedule, whatever room I am in, Ame is always right behind me.

My life is better having her with me wherever we are.

Ame's deliberate "accident" is a sign of how things can go wrong when Aussies get too attached to their schedule; other Aussies might just give their owners helpful reminders.

A Predictable Angel

Sheila Rankin's Aussie, Angel, will wake up out of a dead sleep for her parents' ice-cream routine.

My Australian Shepherd, Angel, is very routine-oriented. She always wakes me up at 7:30 a.m. To do this, she jumps up on the bed, stands on my chest, and licks my face. When that doesn't work, she paws at the covers, trying to pull them off of me. I don't even bother setting an alarm anymore.

Once I'm dressed, I put Angel outside while I get her breakfast ready, then I let her in. She gets a morning treat for coming right back in. If I forget to give her the treat, she reminds me by going to the cabinet and opening it herself.

She is ready to go to sleep at 10 p.m. I put her outside, get ready for bed, and let her back in. Once again, she gets a treat for being a good girl and coming right back in, and if I forget, she reminds me again.

Photo Courtesy of
Shelia Rankin

Another way Angel shows her preference for a strict schedule is if my husband says the words "ice cream." She can be sound asleep, and somehow, she will still hear this. She'll jump up, walk to the freezer, and wait for my husband to get the ice cream out. Then she looks at me to make sure I am getting up, and she looks up at the cabinet where the bowls are. I'll get the bowls out, and my husband will dish out the ice cream and give her one scoop. After her ice-cream treat, Angel will lie back down. She is very predictable!

Angel keeps her owners on a predictable schedule, and so does our next Aussie, but with a little bit more of an attitude.

Everything is All About Her

Loren Taylor's Aussie is one of four pups, and she knows to wait her turn, even if she doesn't like it.

I have four dogs, and everything I do is based on a routine. Otherwise there would be chaos all of the time. Our night routine is probably the best example of this. Harley, our Australian Shepherd, will not go in her crate for bed until after all of our evening rituals are finished.

This is how it usually goes: we have a 1-year-old German Shepherd named Loki that drinks way too much water. She loves to hog the water bowl for herself. In order to allow the others to get water

Photo Courtesy of
Loren Taylor

before bed (just a sip after their last zoomies for the evening), I give them all a treat and make them do tricks (sit, paw, spin, etc.)

Harley knows how to do tricks, but she has learned the order in which I ask her to do them. So, if I have a really good treat like cheese, she does all the tricks before I can even ask her. Or she will do her tricks when I ask a different dog to do the same trick.

After treat time, I walk into the bathroom, grab the water bowl, give Loki about 10 laps of water, then put her in her crate for the evening. While Loki is drinking, Harley is scrounging for extra treats (if I left the closet door open). Otherwise she just stands behind me and stares at me with an impatient face, waiting with attitude for her turn.

Once Loki is in her crate, I go back to the bathroom, grab the water bowl (with Harley and one of the other pups in tow), and place it on the floor. Harley spins around until I get the bowl on the floor, which is usually about one or two excited rotations.

After all of this is finished and she gets her drink, Harley will happily go in her crate and settle in for the night. You can tell that she's waiting for her turn at water and treats, but she certainly isn't happy about it. Everything is all about her!

Harley's routine keeps her in line, and our next Aussie keeps her owner on top of her chores.

Like Hitting Snooze on an Alarm Clock

Jori Caswell tells us about Zoe's farm routine, and how if she's behind on her chores, Zoe will remind her every 10 minutes.

My Aussie, Zoe, is almost two years old, a black tri-color, and small in size (about 32 pounds), but she is not small in personality! I've had her since she was eight weeks old, and she is my first Aussie. She is extremely sweet, a little intense, and very, very observant. If a chair is out of place on the deck or my niece's car seat is sitting in the hallway, where it's never been before, Zoe notices and approaches cautiously to determine if it's a situation she needs to handle or if it's nothing to worry about.

Every day, Zoe, her Golden Retriever sister, Mandy, and I do chores in the morning, late afternoon, and nighttime. Exactly what time we go out varies slightly with the seasons; for example, in the winter we go out a little earlier because it gets dark earlier. Zoe seems to adjust to these slight changes without a problem. I think she partly bases chore time on the amount of daylight because sometimes when it's cloudy or stormy, she will tell me it's time to go out earlier than usual.

Photo Courtesy of
Jori Caswell

When it is time to do chores, Zoe comes and sits about six feet away from me, pricks her ears, looks at me intently, and whines softly. If I'm busy or can't get out to do chores right on time, and tell her, "In a few minutes," she will generally lie down nearby then remind me every 10 minutes or so (by whining at me) that we still haven't gone out. It's sort of like hitting snooze on an alarm clock!

She knows that I usually go down to the basement to get my boots, coat, and any other outerwear that I might need. Then I will exit the basement door and generally go across the gravel road in front of our house to feed the horses, barn cats, and chickens. Zoe knows many phrases like "Let's go get hay for the horses!" and will dash around the front of the barn to the doors where we get hay.

When I tell her we're "going up the hill," she knows that means we are crossing the road and going up the hill behind the house to the second chicken coop. (I keep free-range chickens for eggs and entertainment.) She has a good understanding of which pens/buildings she is and isn't allowed into, and she gets along well with all of the farm animals.

As long as she has enough exercise (physically and mentally), Zoe can handle a little disruption to her schedule, but she definitely prefers a routine. I still have a few things I'm working with her on, but in general, she has been a wonderful addition to the farm and has made me an Aussie fan!

***

Clearly, Australian Shepherds thrive on a routine. Some will learn to count their treats or to tell time so they can keep their owners on the schedule. While it may be annoying on days when a dog owner wants to sleep in or switch up things, predictability in a pet's days help their owners stay on top of chores. You can always feed the dog and slip back under the covers, as long as you don't usually schedule a walk right afterwards.

When adopting a dog, especially one that is borderline obsessive compulsive, think about your household routines. Since your dog will hopefully be part of the family for more than a decade, owners cannot view things in the short term. Once anyone starts serving breakfast at 7 a.m., an Aussie will expect that to unfold every day at the same time. Their days are not as fully scheduled as their humans' are so it's vital to respect that this is how they are wired.

Their awareness of their owners' daily movements is just a glimpse into how attuned Australian Shepherds can be to the people in their lives. Once an owner understands this dynamic, the happier life will be with an Aussie.

Chapter 8:
The Most Sensitive Dog At The Park

Australian Shepherds are very expressive. They have big feelings, and they like to show them. When they're happy, they have bright, beautiful smiles. When they're displeased, they'll let their owners know somehow, whether it's by barking, growling, pouting, or glancing sideways.

Australian Shepherds' intelligence and sensitivity mean that they sometimes react more like humans than your average dog. This can be refreshing and heartwarming. It can also be challenging for humans, especially if an owner is having a bad day and lashes out more loudly than planned. Thankfully, since they are so loyal, they will want to make peace and be friends again, although maybe not right away.

Aussies can become fearful of loud noises, or even a scolding. These sensitive creatures sometimes teach their owners a lesson or two about being more sensitive themselves.

He is My Big Baby

Deb Katz tells us about her Aussie, Rowan Asher, who pouts, whines, and barks when he doesn't get his way.

Rowan Asher is two and a half years old, and he is a lovable, huggable ball of energy. In the morning, when he thinks that it's time to get up and eat his breakfast, he will stand in the bed and stare at me, whining until I open my eyes. He then jumps on and off the bed until

Photo Courtesy of
Deb Katz

I start moving. Sometimes he will actually pull the comforter off the bed. He gets so excited for the day, he will run down the hall, barking the entire time, until he comes into the kitchen and waits to get his breakfast. He started doing this when he was about six months old.

Rowan is very expressive. If he has been told no, he will go sit on the couch and pout and make little whiny sounds, telling me he's annoyed.

The first time he ran to the couch to pout, I had told him "no" about playing with a toy. After whining for a little bit, he got off the couch and threw a toy at me. Then he sat down and picked up his paw, staring at me with his little butt wiggling.

That's generally how it goes now if I tell him no. Couch, pout, whine, throw toys, butt wiggle. If I ignore him, he will start to whine a little bit louder, then he will take the toy and throw it at me again. If I still don't respond, he'll start barking at me while spinning in circles.

He does this most of the time when I'm on a phone call. While I'm talking, he'll start walking around, finding toys. My friends have heard him whining and barking, and they think it's hysterical. He doesn't do this to anyone else—just me.

Rowan loves when people come over because he feels like they're only there to play with him. He will bring toys to them, then sit and wait. Or he'll put his paws on their knees and stare at them until they throw his toys. Everyone gets a kick out of being around him.

He also loves to watch TV when there are other animals on, especially dogs and cats. There was a station called "Dog TV," and he would sit there and watch it, tilting his head back and forth.

Rowan is amazing. When I feel sad, he will come over and put his paws on me and his head on my shoulder. He's my big baby. I don't know what I would do without him!

Rowan Asher isn't the only Aussie who is too sensitive to be told "no." Our next Aussie tries to fix everything with kisses.

A Scolding Leads to a Nibble-Kiss

Loren Taylor tells us how her Aussie, Harley, reacts to scolding.

I have four dogs, and Harley is definitely the sensitive one out of them. If Harley is in trouble and you scold her, she jumps up to reach your face so she can give you kisses and nibble your nose. This makes it impossible to scold her when she is being so cute! Thankfully, she is a good dog 98 percent of the time.

We still haven't figured out how to work around her sensitivity. The other day, Harley jumped on my lap to say hi. She kissed me like she usually does, and I grabbed her to snuggle with her. Well, she didn't want to snuggle, so she kissed me. But in reality, she almost bit my lip.

Photo Courtesy of Loren Taylor

She kind of gives you a snappy-kiss-love-nibble. I told her firmly, "NO. NO bite." That only made the whole situation worse, because then she tried to nibble and kiss even more parts of my face because I'd scolded her. It doesn't hurt, but it's a no-win situation. If you ignore her when she's bad, then she does the nibble-kiss thing. If you grab the back of her scruff to calm her down, it works when you're holding her. But once you release your grip, she'll go back to nibble-kisses.

We have learned never to blow in her face as she is very, very quick and will jump up and nibble-kiss you before you're ready for it. She either hates it or loves it, and either way, it gets her all excited.

Harley overloads her owners with cuteness to get out of a scolding, while our next Aussie mopes and hides.

His Sensitivity is a Blessing in Disguise

It's the end of the world when Evie Hanson's Aussie, Aristotle, hears two words: "Bad dog."

Photo Courtesy of Evie Hanson

When Aristotle was a puppy, I started to notice he was sensitive. Whenever he was scared or hurt, he would immediately look for me. If I was upset and crying, he would rush over to lick my face. He just wants you to be as happy as he is.

Whenever Aristotle acts up or does something bad, we can't use the term "bad dog," or else it is the end of the world. He will mope around all day with his ears down. He will hide, and he will not even look at us. His whole goal in life is to make us happy and love us, so when he's scolded, he takes it so hard.

He loves being the golden dog compared to his sister, Boo. When Aristotle is the one being scolded, he has a whole pity party. And when Boo acts up, Aristotle will come to her defense. He doesn't like us scolding her either, or he takes it personally for some reason.

He will also mope if we yell, "Aristotle!" instead of "Ari." Just like a child, he knows he's in trouble when we use his full name. The only thing that will bring him out of a moping session is treats and playtime.

His sensitivity is a blessing in disguise. He's taught us how to be better about being sensitive to others. Even though he's now almost three, his sensitivity lets us remember how he was as a puppy!

Aristotle's sensitivity makes his owners more sensitive in turn, and our next Aussie reminds his owner not to take his bad moods too seriously.

An Old Soul

Jim Staub tells us of Mouse, an empathetic Aussie who senses mood changes.

Mouse is 10 years old. He is good-natured and wouldn't hurt a soul, but he is also exuberant. When he gets excited, he barks, squeals, and jumps up. At the same time, he's laid-back when no dogs or other people are present. He is also highly intelligent.

Sometimes I think he's an old soul. He can be lying on the floor, and I'll find him staring at me as if he knows something I don't. He always picks up on the emotions of those in the room.

I lost my wife Amy four years ago to breast cancer. Before Amy was sick, Mouse was not as focused on our moods. When Amy got really sick, he stayed beside her. He would sleep with her, not wandering away from her side, even at night. She passed away early in the morning in her sleep, and he must have sensed something was different. Mouse came into my bedroom and woke me up. He wasn't overly excited, but he was insistent that I get up.

He never seemed to get depressed at her passing, but he definitely knows about the loss because now he sticks close, as if he's glued to me.

If I'm in a good mood and in the house, Mouse relaxes near me, but he is always attentive. If I'm sitting at the computer or watching TV

Photo Courtesy of
Jim Staub

and I get up, he's up, too, and wants to see what is next. If I'm sitting for a while, he might go somewhere else and fall asleep. But once I get up, he watches me to see where I am going. While I cook, he stays near me in the kitchen. The only time he is not near me in the house is at night. Once I turn the light out, he goes elsewhere in the house.

Outside, he wants to play Frisbee or wander around the yard sniffing. But he always keeps me in his sight. I have taken him to some drag races, and he will still not leave my side. If I try and let someone else have his leash, he won't go with them.

I've been dating my girlfriend Shari for two years. Mouse is always excited to see her; he'll play outside with her, and he'll play with her when I take him to the races with me. But inside the house, when Shari is around, he is constantly hovering by me, closer than normal. If Shari and I are sitting on the couch, Mouse gets a bit restless. He will move near me, then over to her side, then he will jump up on the couch and put his front paws on the back of the couch as if he wants to jump over the back of it. He'll also stand on his back paws, with his front paws over the half-wall leading into the kitchen, while we're having dinner so he can watch us at our level and be a part of our meal.

I think it's partly his empathy. It's like he senses Shari's higher energy level, and he gets ramped up, whereas I'm a little more laid-back, so he's more relaxed around me. Mouse can also pick up on Shari's mood changes, like when she gets a phone call and it's not good news.

If I'm in a bad mood, he looks at me as if something is wrong. If I swear, he immediately is in my face. If I swear too loudly, he jumps back, and I have to tell him it's okay. Mouse's sensitivity makes it hard for me to release my emotions at times, but I'm glad to have him there to remind me not to take life too seriously.

Mouse's moods and behaviors tend to mirror those he is with, whereas our next Aussie wasn't afraid to let his owners know when he was displeased.

His Sideways Glances Said It All

Michelle Radford-Garris tells us about her Aussie, Cooper, and how he was able to communicate everything with his eyes.

Cooper was the most no-nonsense dog I have ever been around, yet he was still loving and affectionate. He wasn't needy. He didn't like to be petted all the time, but he just wanted to be close to us. He felt like watching over us was his job.

Cooper grinned when he was happy. When I would come home from work or go out to the barn, he would wag his little nub of a tail and grin. It always melted my heart! Cooper loved me. He knew my emotions and how to nuzzle me if I was sad or having a bad day.

However, Cooper didn't like other dogs in his space (even our Beagle, Cricket, that was with us before we got him). He would usually turn his head and look at me sideways when Cricket or other dogs would get in his space with an expression of "Really, Mom? Get them away from me." He might even give a low growl to warn the other dogs. If they didn't listen the first time, he would sometimes give them a snap. As he got older, he became more like a crotchety old man and liked to be bothered even less often.

He was furious the day we went to pick up a new sister for him. That day, I loaded Cooper and Cricket in the truck, and we went to pick the new dog up. All the way there, Cooper was sitting up in the seat, watching the scenery go by, wagging his tail or smiling when I would talk to him in the back seat. Once we got to the location to pick up the pup, I told the dogs I would be right back, and he laid down.

After visiting a while, I brought Annie Oakley (our new pup) back to the truck, opened the door, and put her in. She immediately jumped in the back seat with Cooper. He sat up, looked at me, looked at her, and growled. I fussed at him, and he turned all the way around and looked out the back window. I could see him in my rear-view mirror, and he would look sideways at Oakley, then at me and back out the

Photo Courtesy of
Michelle Radford

window. If the puppy bothered him too much, he would growl at her. I would fuss at him again, and he would scoot as far as possible against the door to stay away from her.

All the puppy wanted to do was play with him. Cooper was excited to get home and out of the truck, away from her. He took one last glance at me and took off to the porch, as far away from Oakley as possible.

Over time, Cooper learned to tolerate her. It took a couple of weeks before I could leave her outside with him without getting snapped or growled at. I always scolded him, and he would give me that sideways look! He quit being ugly to her and would tolerate a tiny amount of playing, but he was nine years old when we got Oakley and was never really into playing, even when he was a puppy. Just no-nonsense, as if he was always saying, "Let me do my job and I'm good."

I believe he forgave me because he knew he was always my special dog. He slept beside my bed every night, while Oakley and Cricket stayed in the basement. Cooper loved that special time with me, and he would grin as he walked past the basement stairs to lie down by my bed.

There will never be another Cooper, and no other dog has ever talked to me with his eyes like he did.

***

Because Australian Shepherds were bred to be caretakers and herders of living creatures, that sensitivity to their surroundings is an invaluable tool. When it comes to a non-working scenario, they become extremely perceptive about their owners and their homes.

This can be a challenge for some owners, whose Aussies might think it's the end of the world when they disappoint their owners. They can convey this with their eyes and body language, clearly letting their owners know if their feelings are hurt.

Knowing this, owners need to make sure they discipline their pets appropriately. Yelling at a dog or hitting them is unnecessary when they read tone of voice and actions so well. Clear communication with a firm 'no' will typically do the trick, as long as you are consistent. If owners soften up and change the rules, it only becomes confusing for a smart dog like an Aussie when it's okay to beg for food, for example, one day but not the next.

Regardless of how they show their sensitivity, most owners would agree that having a caring Australian Shepherd is a blessing.

Chapter 9:

Hoarders Of Toys

Just as Australian Shepherds are very protective of their humans, they can also be very protective of their toys and other high-value items.

Hoarding, guarding, and being possessive of toys is a behavior that is said to originate from when dogs' ancestors didn't have regular access to food. These wild dogs would take food and bury it in a safe place for later, which could mean the difference between life and death in the wild. Translated to modern times, when dogs have access to food, shelter, and all the toys that they could ever want, they may still be resistant to sharing things that they consider to be valuable.

The Australian Shepherd is no stranger to hoarding and protecting its own toys, items it might sneak away from its owner, or toys it may take from its cat or dog friends. This can be frustrating in a multi-dog household. Still, most Aussie owners would agree that it's quite an endearing trait.

She Carries Her Toys Wherever She Goes

Donna Clifford tells us of Layla, her Aussie, who carries around her favorite toys from room to room.

Our Aussie, Layla, is a pack rat. Generally, she's a sweet dog who is very attuned to our emotions and is always at our side. She is a cuddler, and her feelings get hurt easily. She gets along great with other dogs and is very gentle with smaller animals. But when it comes to her toys, she really doesn't like to share them. She's not aggressive about it, but if our other dog (a Sheltie) tries to take her toy, Layla will wait until he puts it down, or she will gently take it from his mouth and carry it out of the room with her.

My sister gave Layla a tough squeaky bone toy as a gift when we were watching her dog for her. After my sister's dog left to go back home, Layla carried that toy everywhere. It became her go-to toy. It has never left her side since; she even takes it to bed with her at night. It is a little worn now, but every time my sister brings her dog

Photo Courtesy of
Donna Clifford

over to visit or stay with us, Layla will bring her that toy and parade it around to make sure everyone sees her prized possession. It doesn't matter where it is in the house or how far down in the toy box it is— she will find it!

Layla always carries a toy with her as she moves from room to room, following us. Most days, it is the one my sister gave her, but every now and then she changes it up.

She often sits outside the bathroom waiting for me. One morning, I exited the bathroom to find a pile of our Sheltie's toys outside the door, and Layla greeting me with her prized possession for the day: our Sheltie's favorite plaything. She was immensely proud of herself for finding it, and it became her treasured toy to carry around for the next couple of days.

She sleeps in bed with us, and we often wake up in the morning to a bed full of toys that she has gathered throughout the night.

Layla isn't the only Aussie who steals and guards toys. Our next Aussie is a bit of a (sweet) bully when it comes to her favorite playthings.

Angel the Bully

Sheila Rankin tells us how her Aussie, Angel, won't share her toys with her German Shepherd "nephew."

Our Aussie, Angel, likes to keep all of her toys and her people near her. Angel is generally a loving and easygoing dog. However, she has a real problem with sharing her toys when her "nephew" (my daughter's dog, Barrett) comes to visit.

Barrett is a three-year-old, 130-pound German Shepherd. He is very laid-back and doesn't growl, bark, or play rough at all. Barrett is basically a big baby.

When Barrett comes to visit, Angel will grab her toys and growl at him. All the while, she will be wagging her stub tail. She loves him,

Photo Courtesy of
Shelia Rankin

but she makes it clear that she does not want him to mess with her toys. With her barks and growls, Angel tries to bully Barrett into staying in one spot so he can't get to her toys. While he's in the house, and she hasn't forced him into a corner, Angel refuses to put her toys down. She will carry at least one toy with her everywhere she goes to make sure Barrett can't get to it.

The funny thing is, if there aren't toys around, or if they're worn out from playing, the two dogs will lie down nicely by each other, like old friends.

Angel bullies her nephew, while our next Aussie steals toys from her cat brother.

Every Toy Belongs to Chloe

Jacklyn Thymian tells us of Chloe's affinity for all toys, especially the ones that belong to the cat.

Photo Courtesy of Jacklyn Thymian

My Aussie Chloe is a pack rat for sure. Every toy is Chloe's, even the cat's toys.

Chloe has always liked cat toys, even when she was a puppy. I think she loves the crinkle sound they make. Chloe and our cat Calvin are best friends, but everything in the house belongs to Chloe, according to her.

When Calvin gets a new toy, he gets to play with it for a little while, but once it looks like too much fun, Chloe will come take it from him. She then goes to her bed and guards it. She will growl at Calvin, but she has never tried to bite him or hurt him. She's never even shown her teeth. Chloe just wants to make it clear that the toy is hers now.

Calvin gets to play with his toys when Chloe is sleeping or just gets bored, but otherwise the toys belong to her. Chloe won't destroy his toys; she just likes to guard them.

Chloe also loves tennis balls. All the tennis balls in the house are her property, especially when other dogs are around. She gets all of them and brings them to her bed.

She will also pick up two bones at a time and bring them to her bed to guard them from other dogs.

Chloe might go after cat toys and tennis balls, but our next Aussie steals some less conventional items.

Ridge the Shoplifter

Debra Padden tells us about Ridge's stealthy habit of stealing arts and crafts items.

Ridge is about a year and a half old. He is classified as a mini-Australian Shepherd, but there is nothing miniature about his personality. He is a beautiful Red Merle and draws a lot of attention for his striking good looks. He also is very smart, and he knows many words (and chooses, on his own accord, which ones he'll listen to). My husband

Photo Courtesy of
Debra Padden

and I are retired, so I wanted a dog to keep us moving and enjoying being outside. Ridge does that for sure!

Ridge is a pack rat by nature, and he steals all kinds of goodies. My husband Larry has a woodworking shop in our basement, and I am a maker of primitive crafts. We refer to our respective woodworking and craft areas as "Harbor Freight" and "Hobby Lobby," and this is where Ridge's "shoplifting" occurs.

Ridge will usually swipe whatever might be on the floor. He steals pieces of wood, spools of thread, jars of paint, etc. He likes to take small items that he can dangle in front of us to let us know what his accomplishment of the day has been! On occasion if we fail to play the game of retrieving the pilfered item in time, he will chew on his prize, but it's really about letting us see his conquest and telling us what he has done. We laugh about how stealthy he can be.

This year I decorated a primitive twig fence out front with big plastic ornaments and old ice skates for Christmas. The ornaments had been residing in "Hobby Lobby" and had garnered quite a lot of Ridge's attention. Each day I would say, "Not Ridge's. Leave it!", and he was surprisingly good about it. However, the temptation once the ornaments were hung on that fence—using bright red yarn, in his yard—was too much. Let's just say all of the ornaments didn't make it back to Hobby Lobby.

He also insists on taking something out to the truck with him when we're going somewhere. It doesn't really matter what it is: a toy, a shoe, a magazine—anything he can grab on his way out the door. Sometimes he'll bring these items back in, but most of the time he just leaves his prizes in the back seat until we clean it out.

Ridge is a lot of fun, but he is also a handful!

Ridge's shoplifting habit is an endearing one, as is our next Aussie's habit of putting her own toys away.

Put Your Toys Away, Rio

Jeff Hutchinson and his wife Sheryl have trained their Aussie, Rio, to put her many toys away at night.

Rio has been an only child since our other dog died about a year ago, so she has lots of toys. At night, she gets a treat if she puts them back in the toy basket.

My wife Sheryl started teaching Rio to put away toys when she was young. It took Rio only about four or five days to start to understand. Sheryl would get some treats. She'd say "take it" to get Rio to pick up the toy and hold it in her mouth. Then she'd hold the treat over the basket, and Rio learned that if she dropped the toy into the basket, she'd earn the treat.

Now, Sheryl just tells Rio to put her toys away, and if she does, Rio gets a bone with peanut butter. Usually we have to tell her, "Put your toys away," then she'll start. Or she'll wait until she sees that we're

Photo Courtesy of Jeff Hutchinson

preparing her bone. But really, it doesn't have anything to do with the peanut butter. It's more that they're her toys, and she likes having them lie around in the living room, so she'll wait until she absolutely has to put them away.

The toy she's most concerned about is her ball. It's the first thing she looks for when she gets up in the morning, and sometimes she'll even take it to bed with her at night. Occasionally, she'll even fall asleep with the ball in her mouth.

The other night, Sheryl started to clean out the toy basket. Some toys were worn out. She told Rio things like, "You haven't played with this one in a long time." She placed those toys in a grocery bag. When she got up to go into the kitchen, Rio took them out of the grocery bag and put them back in the basket. Now, that's a pack rat!

***

Australian Shepherds' pack-rat nature may have developed as a result of their ancestors' time in the wild, but modern Aussies take that trait to a whole new level when it comes to their toys and other prized possessions.

While it may be adorable at first, this can become a behavior that owners may regret allowing if a dog becomes too protective or obsessive with certain items. Be careful what turns into a game since an Aussie's remarkable memory will recall the rules if its owner tries to change them. Just imagine having a fun game of keep-away every day, then finding out you get in trouble for playing it!

Lay out the ground rules early and stick with them. Since Aussies love routine, once they figure out what's permitted and what is not, they will play right along. Whether they're neat and tidy with their toys, or stealthy and adorable thieves, these Australian Shepherds know how to protect their belongings. Just make sure it's clear what they can keep and what they need to share.

Conclusion

Whether you started this book as a first-time owner of an Australian Shepherd or as an already die-hard Aussie fan, you will have come to know and love the stories that each of these owners has shared about their experiences. There's a little bit of truth about each Aussie in the characteristics the owners have described.

As we have learned, Aussies are highly intelligent, and make excellent companions—almost as if you have another human in the family who can help you with chores and take commands with little to no training. These full-time companions can stick to your side like Velcro, whether you're in the bathroom, cooking dinner, or having a bad day and just need a hug.

If you've already brought home your Aussie, you know that these pups have endless amounts of energy. (If you haven't brought one home yet: good luck when you do!) Because they were bred to work, they will find something and make it their job, whether it's keeping track of you 24/7, herding animals on a farm, or playing all day.

One trait that is common among all Aussies is their 100% devotion to their owners. They show it in different ways, but these dogs are so faithful, they would move heaven and earth (or all of your shoes) to keep you near them, safe and happy. These loyal, quick-learning pups will make it their life's work to protect you from any danger, whether it's a service person visiting your house or a real threat of attack. They also like to protect their belongings, and hoard and pack their toys and (sometime-stolen) treasures away.

An Aussie owner should be prepared to have a schedule—and to stick to it—because Aussies love having a routine and a structured day. This could mean never having to set an alarm again because you'll be awakened with Aussie affection. Or it could mean the end of lazy days because your Aussie will boss you around and tell you when it's time to do chores. They will be sensitively attuned to your every move, although they may be reluctant to share their toys.

But what having an Aussie really means is that you will have a loving, affectionate dog who is by your side through thick and thin. Your Aussie will remind you that being kind is the only way to move through life. Aussies will protect you. They will guard you, and they will love you with every fiber of their fluffy beings.

Made in the USA
Middletown, DE
02 January 2022

57497974R00066